Socialism

Key Concepts in Political Theory

Socialism

Peter Lamb

polity

First published in 2019 by Polity Press

Polity Press
65 Bridge Street
Cambridge CB2 1UR, UK

Polity Press
101 Station Landing
Suite 300
Medford, MA 02155, USA

ISBN-13: 978-1-5095-3160-8
ISBN-13: 978-1-5095-3161-5 (pb)

A catalogue record for this book is available from the British Library.
Library of Congress Cataloging-in-Publication Data
Names: Lamb, Peter, author.
Title: Socialism / Peter Lamb.
Description: Medford, Massachusetts : Polity Press, 2019. I Series: Key
   concepts in political theory I Includes bibliographical references and index.
Identifiers: LCCN 2019009980 (print) I LCCN 2019012321 (ebook) I ISBN
   9781509531639 (Epub) I ISBN 9781509531608 I ISBN 9781509531608
   (Hardback) I ISBN 9781509531615(Paperback)
Subjects: LCSH: Socialism.
Classification: LCC HX21 (ebook) I LCC HX21 .L375 2019 (print) I DDC
   335--dc23 LC record available at https://lccn.loc.gov/2019009980

Typeset in 10 on 12pt Sabon
by Fakenham Prepress Solutions, Fakenham, Norfolk NR21 8NL
Printed and bound in Great Britain by CPI Group (UK) Ltd, Croydon

For further information on Polity, visit our website:
politybooks.com

Contents

To Val, my sister, brother, sisters and brothers-in-law, nieces and nephews

Acknowledgements

I thank the many people who have helped me to learn and think about socialism, particularly George Potts, David Morrice, Geraint Parry, Val Lamb and Ian Brown. Thanks also to Staffordshire University for time and resources and to my colleagues and students, from whom I have learnt much.

George Owers at Polity Press offered invaluable help and advice. He was particularly kind and understanding about difficulties and delays due to illness. I am also grateful for advice from three anonymous readers and copy-editing by Justin Dyer.

Acknowledgements

1
Introduction

Rich in diversity, socialism nevertheless has at its theoretical base a clear configuration of tenets. Socialism has been and remains a coherent ideology, even though supporters of some of its variants find others distinctly unappealing. This coherence allows the variants to be grouped into a resilient social and political movement striving, since its emergence in the early nineteenth century, to put its tenets into practice. To retain significance, resonance and appeal, this short book concludes, socialism needs to keep but reframe its core principles, abandon some of the baggage which has allowed it to be disparaged and fight the battles of the present.

Socialism is an ideology of the left based on a distinctive combination of three main principles, equality, freedom and community, around which various other principles revolve. The notoriously imprecise political term 'left' emerged in the French revolutionary period. In the new assembly of 1789, campaigners for liberal and egalitarian reform sat at the left of the chamber. Liberalism is based on a defence of individual freedom, which can involve either reform or resistance to change. As it includes radical reformist liberals, the left is thus broader than socialism. 'Left' came to signify radical political ideas, movements and parties seeking wider and more effective participation, social change, various forms of egalitarianism and reform or abolition of capitalism (Lamb, 2016: 521).

Capitalism is a social and economic system based on a combination of three key features: private ownership of property; self-interested pursuit of such property; and the exchange of goods and the market as means of determining prices of services and goods (Saunders, 1995: 3–9). In prioritizing private property ownership, socialists argue, capitalism encourages individualistic acquisitiveness, discourages community-mindedness, entrenches inequality and allows too much individual rather than social freedom.

In response to the financial crisis that began in 2007, capitalism has survived around the globe by means of austerity for the many. While capitalism may recover in the short term, more fundamental is the inability of Planet Earth to sustain capitalist processes, which are exhausting resources, polluting the environment and bringing irreversible geographical change detrimental to the human species, among others. Socialism has been considered as an alternative by some of those enduring austerity along with their sympathizers. Notwithstanding its potential to foster human flourishing, socialism has, however, sometimes been interpreted, formulated and manipulated in ways which have the opposite effect.

A very prominent form of socialism in the twentieth century, especially after Joseph Stalin took control of the theory and practice of communism in the Union of Soviet Socialist Republics (USSR), was Marxism-Leninism. The USSR was founded in 1922 by Vladimir Lenin, with Stalin's assistance, after Lenin's revolutionary seizure of power in Russia in 1917 (Service, 2000: 308–23, 455–61). Marxism-Leninism drew ostensibly on Lenin's ideas, which in turn interpreted those of Karl Marx. In reality, Marxism-Leninism implemented public ownership in the form of a centrally planned and publicly owned economy, was authoritarian in theory and practice, shunned Western democracy and suppressed opposition. Variants of Marxism-Leninism, often referred to simply as communism, emerged around the world, including the People's Republic of China, which, founded by the revolutionary leader Mao Zedong (or Mao Tse-Tung), is one of several communist states still in existence today (Holmes, 2009: 1–13).

The US-based radical Chinese economist Minqi Li, although critical of the abuse and authoritarianism associated with

Marxism-Leninism (which he refers to by the generic 'socialism'), suggests that something valuable can still be retrieved from the ideology. 'Only with public ownership and society-wide planning', he argues, 'could society achieve ecological sustainability without sacrificing the basic needs of the great majority of the population' (Li, 2013: 41). Many radical environmentalists would challenge Li, suggesting instead that a federation of small-scale communities would be far more suitable for the task of surviving the environmental hazards that are already causing irreparable damage. Socialists, moreover, need not rely on top-down guidance. Indeed, there are new opportunities to be explored for people to have a key role in building socialism for themselves. As Leo Panitch and Sam Gindin (2018: 11–16) suggest, in the present period of capitalist decline following the financial crisis, the tendency for activists in a range of countries to widen their activities from protest to involvement in party politics reflects an opportunity to draw on dissatisfaction with contemporary capitalism to revive a genuinely democratic socialism which takes environmental concerns seriously.

Looking back to the early 1990s, however, when capitalism was in the ascendancy and the ecological problems were less obvious, the prospects for socialism appeared grim. It was fashionable to declare that, having undermined itself and been exposed as a fundamentally malign doctrine with little value, socialism was a spent force. The wide variety of its manifestations and what appeared to be contradictions among socialist ideas led some observers, moreover, to the different, but no less damning, conclusion that the term 'socialism' is meaningless (Beecher, 2013: 370). This book offers a very different analysis, contending that socialism remains as a coherent force on the left. This will become evident as the different variants are discussed. Let us first, however, consider ways in which socialists of various hues have responded to the apparent demise of their ideology.

Socialist decline and recovery

In 1989, a large demonstration in Beijing calling for reforms to Chinese communism was quelled when the state resorted to brutality, bloodshed and repression. In the same year, a series of revolutions erupted in the Eastern European Marxist-Leninist states. By the early 1990s, not only had those states fallen but the USSR, which dominated them, had imploded. Whether this reflected weaknesses in Marx's theories became a moot point.

Marx's work revolves around three main nodes: the analysis of capitalism in terms of social class; a theory of historical trajectory; and a movement for emancipation from exploitation (Wright, 1993: 15–21). The notion of exploitation, which Marx formulated in his early work of the 1840s, builds on the broader meaning of the immoral use of other people for a person's or persons' own ends. Marx was concerned more specifically with the use by the property owners in class-divided societies, without appropriate recompense, of the labour of people who need to work to earn a living. He argued that in the labour process of capitalism this occurs either consciously among members of the two classes or systemically as the owning class benefits from exploitation of the proletariat (industrial working class) with varying degrees of recognition that this is happening (Burnham and Lamb, 2019: 101–20). In the latter case, the labour and lives of the proletarians are in a condition of alienation from their work, products and indeed their human nature (Burnham and Lamb, 2019: 67–100). By 'alienation' he meant that they had lost control of productive activity and consciousness that cooperation in such activity is a feature of the human species.

The emphasis on the system, or structure, is a prominent feature of Marxist writing, but the extent to which Marxism-Leninism replaced the capitalist system with one which introduced a new form of exploitation is debatable. Nevertheless, if so, this justifies neither the view which began to circulate in the 1990s that Marxism itself had been undermined nor the argument that socialism in general was in its death throes. Overcoming or at least minimizing exploitation remains a basic goal for socialism. In the twenty-first century, this has led socialism to challenge and be challenged by neoliberalism, which advocates the minimization of restraints on, and regulation of, global capitalism.

This supposed demise of socialism was celebrated by neoliberal thinkers such as Francis Fukuyama who pronounced the end of history, meaning liberal capitalism would henceforth face no significant challenges. 'Socialism', Fukuyama (1992: 106) declared, 'is no more appealing as an economic model for developing countries than it is for advanced industrial societies.' Perhaps more alarming for socialists were views expressed by some of their own political philosophers. 'As a system', André Gorz (1994: vii) announced, for example, 'socialism is dead'.

The alleged advantages of victorious capitalism were not, however, accepted without question. Saral Sarkar (1991), for example, stressed that many people in capitalist developing countries could only dream of the economic living standards of the German Democratic Republic (East Germany), which, he acknowledged, was nevertheless an awful authoritarian regime which wasted natural resources. Change was needed, but capitalism was not the answer. Socialist feminists, too, insisted that the direction of change need not be towards capitalism. Feminism is concerned with the exclusion of women from roles and circumstances which enable empowerment and flourishing. While Marxism-Leninism had not allowed women to flourish, capitalism, against which socialism continued to campaign, was linked with patriarchy, or in other words male domination. Capitalism was thus biased towards the exclusion of women from positions of power (Haug, 1991).

Feminist socialism is one of many variants of the socialist ideology, ranging from the radical revolutionary to the moderate social democratic. Social democrats hold that a form of socialism at least tolerable to people of other ideological persuasions can be introduced by means of regulation, achieved through parliamentary politics. Some social democrats in the early 1990s argued that a revived or resuscitated socialism need not attempt to uproot capitalism but rather could subject it to significant reform and control. In 1994, such a mild social democratic view was voiced by the new British Labour Party leader, Tony Blair.

Blair argued that while the Marxist strand of socialism, based, as he saw it, on central control of industry and production, was dead, the traditional ethical strand was very much alive, albeit in need of revival. As a practising Christian and a member of the Christian socialist movement, Blair thought in terms of family, insisting that individuals were interdependent and social beings, undetachable from their society. This, for him, was the basis of a democratic form of socialism having as its values social justice, the equal worth of citizens, equality of opportunity and community (Seldon, 2005: 516–19).

Hyphenating his position as 'social-ism', Blair (1994: 4) sought to 'move beyond the battle between public and private sector and see the two as working in partnership'. On this basis, the notion of 'The Third Way', or '*Die Neue Mitte*', became popular among theorists such as Anthony Giddens and politicians such as the German Social Democratic Party (SPD) leader Gerhard Schröder. They argued that traditional social democracy, with its focus on nationalized industries and services, was discredited and outdated, as were the obsessively free-market ideas of neoliberalism. To retrieve the ethical tradition, social democracy needed to be thoroughly modernized (Giddens, 1998, 2000). Drawing on the idea of the radical centre which had been circulating in recent political thinking, Giddens (1998: 44–6) stressed that the centre was not necessarily moderate. The centre could propose substantial social change, the appeal of which would not be restricted to the traditional right or left. The Third Way achieved considerable electoral results in Europe. Having distanced himself from the principle of common ownership of the means of production, distribution and exchange and styled his party as New Labour, for example, Blair won three successive general elections.

Nevertheless, the electoral success of the modernized social democracy did not mean that henceforth the ideological spectrum would extend no further to the left. Even before the Third Way was pronounced, there were signs that socialism might have a radical future. At the end of 1994 in Chiapas, southern Mexico, for example, activists of the Zapatista movement suddenly took direct revolutionary action against the Mexican capitalist state, catching the attention of people unattracted to the old forms of socialism. Reflecting later upon the appearance of his movement, the charismatic, masked Zapatista leader who styled himself Subcomandante Marcos (2004: 5–6) stressed that there had been 'two major gaps in the movement of the revolutionary Left in Latin

America'. First, there were the indigenous peoples from whom his movement had emerged. Second, there were minorities such as LGBT people who were not only excluded from the discourses of the Latin American left but also disregarded and sometimes even opposed by communist parties.

The Zapatistas helped inspire a campaign against global capitalism. The anti-capitalist movement gained momentum after the famous 'battle in Seattle' of 1999, when thousands of protesters demonstrated outside a meeting of the World Trade Organization (WTO) (Callinicos, 2003: 4–5). Particularly in Latin America, considerable support grew for left-wing parties and movements, some of which went on to win political office and power. Some were radical, such as those in Venezuela and Bolivia led by Hugo Chávez and Evo Morales, respectively (Burbach, 2014). Others were more moderate, such as the Workers' Party in Brazil led by presidents Luiz Inácio Lula da Silva (Lula) and Dilma Rousseff, which nevertheless achieved reforms that were impressive considering the oppressive conditions in the country before their election to government (Morais and Saad-Filho, 2011). After the end of history had been declared, socialism had thus begun to stage a range of significant revivals. The wide variety within socialist ideology in this short period, moreover, reflected the richness it had exhibited throughout its history.

As is the case with any ideology, theory, on the one hand, and experience of political activity, on the other, have a reciprocal influence. An emerging example of such a linkage was identified by Ralph Miliband (1994: 194–5), who, in *Socialism for a Sceptical Age*, argued that the present age had become one of 'wild capitalism', wherein gross inequalities and austerity were accepted as normal. This ethos and the conditions it sought to justify would not, he opined, be tolerated now that a revolution in communications had made people far more aware of their world and better able to organize. The ongoing developments in communications since he wrote have indeed fostered new forms of politics, discourse, organization and action. Nevertheless, socialists must face the reality that information and communications technology is used very effectively by their opponents. Reflecting on what the revival of social democracy had and had not achieved, Tony Fitzpatrick (2003: 61–71) discussed the commodification of information, and the strengths of employers, especially large corporations, in this respect. In other words, information was perceived in terms of profit and loss and workplace surveillance had increased with information technology. Internet activity and the use of email had made the lives of workers and consumers far easier to track. Information about workers was valuable to ensure their work practices were not too expensive, while information about consumers could be used to sell them more goods and services. Exploitation had extended to transforming human thought and action into a series of binary-coded decisions that simplify human relations. Marx (1977: 61–74) had written in the 1840s that the capitalist system alienated humans from their labour, their selves and their species. With the commodification of information and the freeing of industry from systematic organization and accountable authority, this alienation had only intensified.

As Gorz (1994: 38–41) noted, few people now desired systematic organization of their lives; but they still sought emancipation, by means of which they could achieve self-development and self-determination collectively, through solidarity and cooperation, in an ecologically sustainable society. Whilst, as mentioned above, he conceded that socialism had died as a system, this did not, for him, mean that socialism was dead *per se*.

To survive and flourish, socialism would need to move with the times. It was not enough, Marx (1968a: 30) had famously stated in his 'Theses on Feuerbach' of 1845, to interpret the world as had the philosophers; the world needed to be changed. As Boris Kagarlitsky (2000: 148) suggested, however, in *The Return of Radicalism* : 'To change the world the left has to change itself.'

Whilst early twenty-first-century instances of socialist revival combined original principles and consistent goals with new ideas and innovative strategies, reversals sometimes followed. These reversals were not restricted to the radical sections of the socialist movement. Indeed, if the moderates felt comfortable in the belief that their social democracy was safe, they would soon receive a rude awakening. The global financial crisis of 2007–8 compelled European social democrats in government and opposition to rethink their plans.

Although the crisis was widely considered to have disturbed the very foundations of capitalism, European socialism was not ready to offer a swiftly applicable alternative. Marxism-Leninism had been discredited and moderate socialists who sought the gradual reform of capitalism now appeared complacent. Many social democratic and labour parties supported or at least tolerated some degree of austerity (Sassoon, 2014: xviii). Even some of the more firmly established moderate parties suffered as their popularity declined. The British Labour Party, for example, lost power and entered a long period of opposition.

Nevertheless, some of the radical socialist movements in Europe now became parties and attracted considerable support, notably Podemos in Spain and SYRIZA in Greece – the latter even forming the elected government (Smaldone, 2014: 305–7). In the UK, the left-winger Jeremy Corbyn was elected leader of the Labour Party in 2015. Labour subsequently gained sizeable support, especially among young people, over the next few years (Whiteley et al., 2019). Although insufficient for the purposes of winning the general election of 2017, this revealed that radical socialism may have a future (Panitch and Gindin, 2018: 65–80). Similarly, in 2016, the self-declared socialist Bernie Sanders surprised many in the USA by the size and enthusiasm of his support, especially among young voters, in his bid to be the Democratic Party's presidential candidate. Although he was unsuccessful, Sanders' ability to connect was remarkable in a country where socialism rarely enjoyed more than very minor levels of support (Panitch and Gindin, 2018: 41–6).

By that time, however, the Latin American revival appeared to have run out of steam. In Brazil, Rousseff was impeached, Lula was jailed for alleged wrong-doing, and in 2018 the right-wing Jair Bolsonaro was elected president. In Venezuela, Chávez's successor, Nicolás Maduro, struggled to maintain control amidst mass campaigns against his authoritarian rule and the collapse of the economy of this oil-rich country (Cárdenas, 2014). In Greece, for all its radical beginnings, SYRIZA was compelled to adopt austerity policies after its election to government in 2015, finding this necessary to gain financial support from the European Union and the

International Monetary Fund (IMF) (Karyotis and Rüdig, 2018: 167). SYRIZA was criticized by some to its left for capitulating. Attempting radical change may, however, have led to far greater economic and social problems for the working class and other disadvantaged Greek people (Panitch and Gindin, 2018: 53–63). While new socialist movements and parties with radical ideas could achieve some progress, the defenders of the capitalist order would not relax their grip upon economic power.

Indeed, a quarter of a century after the collapse of Marxism-Leninism in the USSR and Eastern Europe, Axel Honneth suggested in *The Idea of Socialism* that while socialism could still attract strong, enthusiastic support, this was nevertheless still far too limited. Socialism, according to Honneth (2017: viii), 'still contains a vital spark, if only we can manage to extract its core idea from the intellectual context of early industrialism and place it in a new socio-economic framework'. Socialism has in fact always evolved and been reformulated in response to changing circumstances, thus remaining an irritant to the vested interests of capitalism.

We have so far glanced at recent developments and at some of socialism's problems and prospects. Later this introductory chapter will peruse the history of socialist forms and ideas and the contexts in which they were developed. First, however, a key concept already mentioned several times needs to be clarified: ideology.

Socialism as an ideology

The word 'ideology' is used in various ways; sometimes pejoratively to refer to doctrines – including socialist doctrine – considered to be over-zealous. This is very different from the original usage of 'ideology' by Antoine Destutt de Tracy to refer to the study of ideas (Freeden, 2003: 4–5). It is rare to find de Tracy's usage echoed in later political writing. The word was used alternatively by Marx to refer to philosophy or doctrines that were misleading and apologetic in seeking to create legitimacy in the service of those they benefit

(Parekh, 1982: 1–14). The interpretation of 'ideology' used in the present study is more widely employed today than any of those just mentioned. Descriptive rather than normative, it is expressed in various ways, three of which will be mentioned here, the third serving neatly to summarize the other two.

The first of these interpretations was formulated in the 1970s by Martin Seliger (1976: 175–208), who suggested that ideologies have two dimensions: the fundamental (ideas, theories, criticisms, etc.) and the operative (political movements, actions, etc.). The operative dimension builds on the fundamental. In their version, Terence Ball and Richard Dagger (1999: 5–9) suggested that ideology has four functions: (1) explanation of why the social, political and economic conditions are the way that they are; (2) evaluation of those conditions; (3) orientation, which enables people to perceive their identities, their position in society and the groups, classes, movements, and so on, to which they belong; and (4) formulating a political programme which prescribes the social and political action to be taken. In the version which serves to summarize the other two, Andrew Heywood argues that an ideology (a) offers an account of the existing order; (b) advances a model of a desired future; and (c) explains how to bring about political change. He summarizes this as follows: 'An ideology is a more or less coherent set of ideas that provides the basis for organized political action, whether this is intended to preserve, modify or overthrow the existing system of power' (Heywood, 2012: 11).

According to Heywood's interpretation, the set of ideas at the basis of an ideology is likely to include views on equality, freedom, community, the state, property and the economy. These are ideas with which socialists are particularly concerned. This set of ideas, linked together as a matrix on which to formulate political strategy, amounts to what Seliger referred to as the fundamental dimension, wherein socialists both explain and evaluate. Furthermore, in Heywood's terms, socialism presents an argument that the existing system of power – the capitalist system – is unreasonable, inappropriate and exploitative and thus should be overthrown or substantially reformed. This can be seen in terms of Seliger's operative dimension. Heywood referred to organized political action. This is what Ball and Dagger meant when they said ideologies such as socialism formulate political programmes. Socialism also provides a coherent rallying point for people who are exploited in the capitalist system to recognize the collective identity they share in their class or group, thus enabling them to join the socialist movement. This coherence, which is a key point of Heywood's version, can be detected as an important aspect of Ball and Dagger's orientation function.

Coherence is, however, rarely total. We have seen that socialism and feminism sometimes overlap one another because they have shared concerns, arguments or goals. This ideological overlapping can also be found between the tenets of socialism and those of liberalism and anarchism. While liberalism is essentially concerned with people as individuals operating in a market economy, their liberties protected by constitutional government, some liberals also believe government should provide welfare for some individuals even though this restricts the private property accumulation of others (Johnston, 2010). The latter form of liberalism overlaps with the social democratic wing of socialism. Anarchism, on the other hand, opposes authority and considers the state as, fundamentally, an instrument of oppression. Some anarchists argue that socialism is possible without a state and consider themselves libertarian socialists or anarcho-communists (Ward, 2004: 1–13).

Ideological overlap is a phenomenon to which this book returns at various places. The examples of such overlapping reflect the environment in which the modern ideologies emerged and developed to promote ways for humans to live in response to the conditions and social arrangements of the modern era. Indeed, it will be useful to remember this point about overlap when, in the following section, similarities between ideologies become apparent as we examine how the socialist ideology emerged and developed in the nineteenth century. After almost two hundred years of further development, the recent and perhaps continuing period of flux is one in which socialism has seemed to be alternately experiencing a demise or a revival.

The emergence and early development of socialism

Attempts are sometimes made to trace the origins of socialism to theorists and activists of ancient Greece, biblical times and early Christianity. Whilst some socialist tenets do indeed have roots and antecedents stretching into the distant past, as a distinctive political movement it only really began to develop during the industrial revolution in the early nineteenth century (Beecher, 2013: 369; Buzby, 2010: 1295; Lamb, 2016: 2–3). Socialism emerged in Western Europe during this period of social upheaval, during which ways of life were subjected to dramatic transformation and moral values underwent radical change (Lichtheim, 1975: 10–26). More precisely, socialism emerged in the 1820s. The Napoleonic Wars had caused economic dislocation and discontent, accentuating the inequalities and inequities of the newly emergent modern capitalism which had fostered the expansion of industry and the development of machinery. The exploitation of working people by their employers and the capitalist system was intensified by the condition of the economy in the years following the defeat of Napoleon (Smaldone, 2014: 20–1). These developments amounted to the new environment in which the socialist movement would emerge, consisting both of people who sought liberation from exploitation and writers who tried to articulate the experiences and demands of those people while also theorizing what should be done in response. Theorists writing during the first two decades of the nineteenth century such as Charles Fourier in France and Robert Owen in the UK would not initially have recognized themselves as socialist – indeed, the term did not come into use until the 1820s. Nevertheless, their ideas became key theoretical foundations of socialism.

Owen argued that human beings will cooperate with one another in their communities if taught and encouraged to do so. Cooperation would become natural to them, just as has competition in modern society because of conditioning. He put this idea into practice at his New Lanark cotton mill in Scotland, where employees and their children were paid well, educated and treated fairly. The success in terms of production and output led him to write *A New View of Society* (1813–16). 'Any general character', he argued, 'from the best to the worst, from the most ignorant to the most enlightened, may be given to any community, even to the world at large, by the application of proper means' (Owen, 1991: 12). Radicalized by his experience, he began to argue for the creation of a society of cooperative villages, which he attempted to build when he emigrated to the USA in the 1820s. Although these projects were unsuccessful, his ideas were hugely influential. Cooperatives – associations whose members worked together for their mutual advantage – had existed in the UK since the mid-eighteenth century and, inspired by Owen's ideas and example, a movement reviving such practice emerged (Lamb, 2016: 105). The word 'socialism' was first used in this movement by the London Co-operative Society in the late 1820s in its *London Co-operative Magazine* (Smaldone, 2014: 31). The cooperative idea gained support throughout the world, leading in 1895 to the formation of the International Cooperative Alliance. Cooperative ideas continued thereafter to feature in various socialist theories and projects.

Socialism developed as an ideology committed to a struggle for emancipation from exploitation, and hence for freedom. The gross inequalities of capitalism were considered unjust. Encouraged by the early thinkers of the ideology, working-class people came to see that exploitation was inherent within the existing social order based on the institution of private property. In their search for an alternative to such a society, the early socialists were more concerned with communal economic cooperation and organization than political institutionalism at the state or any other level (Honneth, 2017: 33–5). The problem was that communal organization is ultimately inconsistent with the smooth workings of capitalism. Thinkers such as Owen tried to persuade the exploitative minority that even they would enjoy better lives if they realized the importance of community to human development. The upheaval required in economic, political and social institutions and practices for such cooperation to become the norm was, however, deemed impractical, especially by those whose interests were upheld by the *status quo*. Hence, according to Owen in *A New View of Society*, it would be futile to turn to existing politicians for help in introducing a new society based on cooperative rather than selfish principles, as the trammels of their parties misled their judgement and constrained them 'to sacrifice the real well-being of the community and of themselves, to an apparent but most mistaken self-interest' (Owen, 1991: 61). Instead, the task should be left to those (including himself, one presumes) who had become conscious of the realities of their existing society, and could 'perceive the inseparable connection which exists between the individual and general, between private and public good!' (Owen, 1991: 61).

The supposition that exploitation would have to be endured was challenged in a very different way than Owen had recommended by the early French socialist Flora Tristan, who in 1843 appealed to workers to club together to form their own union rather than wait to be guided (Tristan, 2007: 37–41). This encouragement for workers to help build their own socialist society was continued just a few years later by Marx and his fellow intellectual from the Prussian Rhineland, Friedrich Engels, who, together in *The Communist Manifesto* of 1848, told the proletarians they had nothing to lose but their chains, and a world to win. 'Working men of all countries unite!' (Marx and Engels, 2002: 258), they wrote at the end of this revolutionary pamphlet.

In the decades that followed, socialism grew as a movement seeking to build a society in which ordinary people would exercise choice over how to achieve human flourishing, utilizing their talents in ways that brought satisfaction in cooperation but without exploiting others. Fellowship or community came to take diverse forms, of which various socialist theorists have offered their views as to which is the best and most appropriate. Fellowship was often considered to extend beyond state boundaries, involving solidarity between exploited people from different countries. Socialism thus became an internationalist ideology, even though in practice it did not match such cosmopolitan expectations.

In their *Manifesto*, Marx and Engels criticized earlier communists such as François-Noel Babeuf, whose ideas were made famous in the *Manifesto of the Equals*, summarized in 1796 by Sylvain Maréchal (1964: 51–5) in revolutionary

France. These pre-Marxian communists were republican, egalitarian and authoritarian, thus differing from early nineteenth-century thinkers who considered themselves socialists. The latter thinkers likewise wanted social and political change for the benefit of ordinary people but were more concerned with association and cooperation (Lichtheim, 1975: 28, 37–8, 58, 60–3). In the 1840s, the German thinker Moses Hess (1964: 272–3) sought to narrow the distinction, arguing that a moral revolution would bring about a social revolution that was realistic in its aims rather than the levelling demanded by early communists. This in turn would lead to a socialism that transcended the earlier communism.

Like Hess, in their *Manifesto*, Marx and Engels (2002: 253) rejected the levelling and universal asceticism of early communism, distancing themselves from the extreme commitment of those early thinkers to equality. Marx and Engels nevertheless called themselves communists rather than socialists. Their idea for the new society was based on the assumption that the productive capacity of capitalist society would be taken over by the proletariat, led by the communists. Their communism advocated 'not the abolition of property generally, but the abolition of private property' (Marx and Engels, 2002: 235). Immediately after the proletarian revolution, capital would be wrested from the defeated bourgeoisie (the class which owned the means of production and capital). The proletariat would 'centralize all instruments of production in the hands of the state' (Marx and Engels, 2002: 243). Productive forces would then be increased so that there would be no need for the asceticism advocated by the early communists. 'In Communist society', Marx and Engels (2002: 236) insisted, 'accumulated labour is but a means to widen, to enrich, to promote the existence of the labourer.' Exploitation would be abolished. As they put it: 'Communism deprives no man of the power to appropriate to products of society; all that it does is to deprive him of the power to subjugate the labour of others by means of such appropriation' (Marx and Engels, 2002: 238).

Later in the nineteenth century, Marxists gradually abandoned the socialist–communist distinction, often referring to their own movement as a socialist one. However, a very prominent division emerged between Marxists and anarchists. This division reflects a difference between anarchism and socialism more broadly, the main point of disagreement being on authority, for which, unlike anarchists, socialists perceive a need. The rejection of authority meant that anarchists were resolutely opposed to the state, which, they believed, because it necessarily perpetuates oppression and tyranny, could not even in the short term be utilized for liberation. Unlike the more individualistic variants of anarchism, collectivist forms of anarchism overlapped with socialism, including Marxism, regarding emancipation, egalitarianism and collectivism. Crucially, however, the anarchists opposed the Marxist argument that a new, temporary form of state was necessary after the revolution to organize society (Marshall, 1993: 24–8). In the mid-nineteenth century, many on the collectivist wing of anarchism joined with Marxists in 1864 in the International Workingmen's Organization (later known as the First International), in which there was bitter rivalry between factions, especially between Marx's wing and Mikhail Bakunin's anarchist faction (Thomas, 1980: 249–340).

The internal divisions led to the First International's demise in 1876. Thirteen years later, the Second International was formed, comprising both Marxist and more moderate parties from within the movement (Geary, 2003). Until the early twentieth century, the parties in each of these two wings often labelled themselves as social democratic. They were, however, very different from one another.

The German SPD was originally Marxist, with Engels, Karl Kautsky and Eduard Bernstein as its prominent thinkers. Engels portrayed Marxism as scientific socialism. 'Just as Darwin discovered the law of development of organic nature', Engels (1968: 429) suggested at Marx's funeral in 1883, 'Marx discovered the law of development of human history.' Marx, he continued, also 'discovered the special law of motion governing the present-day capitalist mode of production and the bourgeois society that this mode of production has created'. Marx did, indeed, sometimes present his ideas in scientific terms, but stressed in his major work *Capital* in 1867 that the 'natural laws of capitalist production' are in fact 'tendencies', and that 'neither microscopes nor chemical reagents are of assistance' in the analysis of economic forms (Marx, 1976: 90).

In *The Communist Manifesto* of 1848, Owen, Fourier and other socialists who had not seen the necessity for revolutionary class struggle were described disparagingly by Marx and Engels (2002: 253–6) as Utopian. In his major work *Anti-Dühring* (a critique of the socialist thinker Eugen Dühring) thirty years later, Engels suggested that the Utopians had perceived what they considered as the truth without recognizing that their views were conditioned by their subjective understandings. 'To make a science of socialism', he argued, 'it had first to be placed on a real basis' (Engels, 1976: 33). He described political economy as a science which was essentially historical, dealing with constantly changing historical material. Before so doing, political economy needed to 'first investigate the special laws of each individual stage in the evolution of production and exchange, and only when it has completed this investigation will it be able to establish the few quite general laws which hold good for production and exchange in general' (Engels, 1976: 187). Although Kautsky (1936: 20) was careful in 1887 to stress the similarities between social and scientific laws rather than portray the former as examples of the latter, the perception of Marxism as scientific became part of late nineteenth-century orthodox Marxism, of which Engels and he were the prominent thinkers.

More recognizably social democratic as we understand the term today, Bernstein published his controversial book *The Preconditions of Socialism* in 1899. Having earlier been a close associate of Engels and Kautsky, Bernstein (1993) argued that Marxism needed to be brought up to date. Marxism would thus, he argued, advocate a slow, democratic transition as possible and indeed more desirable than revolution.

Meanwhile, Christian ethical socialism attracted significant support. In the UK in the late nineteenth century, for example, some socialists organized in the Labour Church movement (Bevir, 2011: 278–97). Religion was also a key feature of the Socialist Party of America (SPA), which from its formation in 1901 until 1934 was a minor but significant actor in US politics, with a membership of up to 118,000 and regular presidential candidacies by its leader, Eugene Debs (Lamb, 2016: 441). The SPA campaigned against capitalism, which activists in the party considered an obstacle to building a cooperative commonwealth as the kingdom of God on earth. The activists portrayed Jesus Christ as a socialist and socialism as religion. For them, a more universal religion needed to replace doctrinal, denominational Christianity (McKanan, 2010). In the 1930s, divisions appeared in the party, undermining its distinctive religious stance. By then, in the UK the Christian socialist strand had been represented most powerfully by R.H. Tawney.

For Tawney, socialists needed to appeal to principles. This, he insisted in *The Acquisitive Society* of 1921, was 'the condition of any considerable reconstruction of society, because social institutions are the visible expression of the scale of moral values which rules the minds of individuals, and it is impossible to alter institutions without altering that valuation' (Tawney, 1961: 10). A problem was that in modern society property rights and self-interest had come to be considered natural, private property being defended on principle from demands based on human need. For Tawney (1961: 13–14), this principle should be replaced by two others. First, 'industry should be subordinated to the community in such a way as to render the best service technically possible'. Second, as a necessary condition of economic freedom (by which he meant freedom at work), the direction and government of industry 'should be in the hands of persons who are responsible to those who are directed and governed'. This, he stressed, was a Christian philosophy of community. Humans, whom God had made equal, had equal rights that were 'a commission of service, not a property' (Tawney, 1961: 185).

In another development in the UK, socialists, including Sidney Webb, Beatrice Webb and George Bernard Shaw, became prominent in the Fabian Society, formed in the 1880s. The name 'Fabian' derives from the tactics of the ancient Roman General Fabius. On the front cover of the very first Fabian tract, *Why Are the Many Poor?*, in 1884, the Society advised socialists to wait patiently and strike hard at the appropriate moment, as Fabius had done in the war against Hannibal (Fabian Society, 1884: 1). The

Fabians were, indeed, confident that socialism would emerge gradually, guided by a strong state at the national level. In his paper 'Transition' in 1888, Shaw (1931) described this process as the transition to social democracy. For him, it made no sense for this not to happen. 'The establishment of socialism, when once people are resolved upon it', he suggested anonymously in the Fabian Society pamphlet *What Socialism Is* two years later, 'is not so difficult as might be supposed.' 'Few', he elaborated, 'now believe Socialism to be impractical except those with whom the wish is father to the thought' (Fabian Society, 1890: 3).

Marxists who described themselves as social democrats included Lenin in Russia. In *What Is to Be Done?* in 1902, he described a conflict between two trends in international social democracy. The first was revolutionary, Marxist social democracy. The second trend, meanwhile, represented by a range of thinkers, including the Fabians and the revisionist Bernstein, sought to change social democracy into a democratic party of bourgeois social reformism (Lenin, 1947: 8–9). This can be rather confusing when one considers the later history of socialism, in which a division has often been drawn in the twentieth and twenty-first centuries between the communist and social democratic wings of socialism.

What brought about the application of the term 'social democracy' exclusively to parliamentary, democratic socialism was the tendency after the Russian revolution of 1917 for Marxist parties to refer to themselves as 'communist' and reformist socialists alone as social democratic. Many moderates did not care for this label and instead called their parties and movements labour, democratic socialist or simply socialist. Nevertheless, most major socialist parties in the world came to be recognized as belonging to one or the other side of this division.

The communist/social democratic division did not mean that each side was homogeneous in terms of the theories that influenced the major thinkers, movements, parties and groups. An important point is that socialist theories often, consciously or otherwise, take into consideration the historical, social and cultural conditions of the country or countries in which their preferred state is intended to be introduced or further developed. Sidney and Beatrice Webb (1920:

310–11) took this approach in response to the Bolshevik revolution of 1917 and contributed to a distinctive British socialist tradition which developed in the 1920s. Prominent in that tradition were Harold Laski and G.D.H. Cole. Their thought combined confidence that people could live cooperatively as associates in voluntary groups (a view known as associationalism) with Fabian ideas of a strong role for the state at the national level (Bevir, 2011: 312). Furthermore, at around the same time, the influential Swedish model of social democracy began to take shape.

Social democratic parties began to link with one another in 1951, through the formation of the Socialist International. Its growing membership came to include an increasingly wide variety of labour, social democratic and radical democratic socialist parties (Lamb, 2016: 16–17, 435–7). Meanwhile diversity on the Marxist-Leninist, communist side emerged. Maoist Chinese Marxism-Leninism, for example, differed significantly from that of Stalin which underpinned and drove the USSR (Holmes, 2009: 7–13).

Mention of the associationalist tradition above indicates that the communist–social democratic dichotomy does not capture every sort of socialist thought. Some socialist movements, groups, parties and the ideas and theories which inspire them do not fit even loosely into either side. In some such cases, the theory does not have a substantial body of support but, rather, aspires to or intends to influence the building of a following in the movement. Alternatively, some such theories are predominantly academic, their thinkers fully expecting any influence to filter down to the socialist movement gradually rather than immediately inspire action at the operative level of the ideology. The rich diversity within socialism in theory and practice will be discussed in the remainder of this book.

Issues in socialism

The historical development just sketched aims to prepare the ground for discussion of some key aspects of socialism, and disputes within the ideology, in the chapters that follow. A wide range of examples will both reflect and illustrate this theoretical diversity of socialism. Each chapter will also illustrate ways in which disagreement – often indeed open hostility – can be found among socialists on the issues in question.

Chapter 2, which immediately follows this introduction, considers the place of freedom, equality and community as concepts in socialist theory. One of the features that distinguishes socialism in different ways from the ideologies with which it overlaps is the distinctive combination of these three concepts. There are various versions of these concepts in socialist theory. Nevertheless, the versions have enough in common to locate them within the same ideology.

Chapter 3 considers socialist views on the state and the economy. Socialism is often portrayed as an ideology which advocates tight state control of the economy. This is especially the case in portrayals offered from opponents of socialism. Some variants of socialism do indeed have such state control as their central feature. Nevertheless, in many other cases there have been different views of both the role of the state and the nature of the socialist economy.

While they all criticize the existing capitalist economy and the role of the state that defends it, socialists have various views on how both the state and economy should change. This focus on requirements for change continues even when socialism becomes quite entrenched in the authoritative control of a country but has yet to achieve the results it sought. Hence, Chapter 4 considers political and social change, in which both diversity and the crucial affinities within the ideology are discussed.

The goals and programmes of some significant socialist examples are discussed in Chapter 5, which examines a range of blueprints for a new society presented by socialists in the twentieth and twenty-first centuries. Once again, diversity and affinities can be found. This is not to suggest that all or even most cases of socialist theory offer a clear vision of the intended new society. Indeed, some socialists have no desire to sketch one. As the chapter will discuss, however, in some notable cases, socialists do have such a clear view and, moreover, have made attempts to put their blueprints into practice.

The concluding chapter considers how the themes discussed in the book can be found in some recent variations within the ideology. The prospects for socialism in a very different world than that in which the ideology emerged and grew will be discussed. Socialism, it will be argued, has survived many setbacks but currently faces challenges and obstacles at least as difficult as those of the past.

2
Freedom, Equality and Community

Socialism in its various forms incorporates a philosophy of equality. Michael Newman (2005: 2) suggests that the 'commitment to the creation of an egalitarian society' is 'the most fundamental characteristic of socialism'. Newman was neither suggesting that egalitarianism is associated exclusively with socialist political philosophy nor overlooking the fact that a range of other ideologies, such as feminism, anarchism and liberalism, are also egalitarian in different ways. Liberalism, for example, is committed to formal equality and equality of equal human worth.

Socialism does indeed have as a core belief a commitment to some degree of egalitarian narrowing of differences in the actual conditions of human beings to enable each to achieve self-development collectively. There are, however, other central features which are no less important to the ideology. First, communitarian fellowship is a state of mind necessary for socialist egalitarianism and its commitment to overcome or reduce exploitation of others – exploitation that, according to socialists, characterizes capitalism, or at least insufficiently regulated capitalism. Without such fellowship, a commitment to equality may be held by another ideology such as liberalism. Second, there is a commitment to a sort of freedom which, socialists argue, is necessary for human flourishing. The socialist commitments to both freedom and equality were expressed very clearly in an influential pamphlet first published in 2010 by Stéphane Hessel. 'History's direction', he insisted, 'is towards more justice and more freedom – though not the unbridled freedom of the fox in a henhouse' (Hessel, 2011: 23). Notwithstanding the diversity within socialism, some variants being considerably more authoritarian than others, by starting with equality we can better understand socialist freedom, community and the other values and tenets.

Socialist equality and community

Some socialists take the egalitarian aspect further than others. Importantly, nevertheless, after the early communists of the late eighteenth and early nineteenth centuries (of whom Marx was later very critical), few socialists have argued that equal treatment involves identical treatment, which would be detrimental to freedom. Most socialists place considerable emphasis on sorts of freedom which, formulated appropriately, can enable equality to develop in more widely acceptable ways.

Seeking to present equality in such terms in the early twenty-first century, G.A. Cohen argued that the relevant equality is a radical version of equality of opportunity. This radical version seeks to correct for all disadvantages 'for which the agent cannot herself reasonably be held responsible, whether they be disadvantages that reflect social misfortune or disadvantages that reflect natural misfortune' (Cohen, 2009: 18). Cohen (2009: 13) called this a principle of 'socialist equality of opportunity', insisting that such inequalities as this principle will permit must not be allowed to become too great. Otherwise, a socialist society would soon revert to a capitalist one. As he suggested, the principle of community is crucial if the socialist society is to avoid such reversion (Cohen 2009: 24–43).

Cohen's criticism of the standard liberal doctrine of equality of opportunity bears affinities to that which R.H. Tawney had offered in the 1930s, albeit in a very different style. In *Equality*, Tawney (1931: 142) portrayed the liberal doctrine as 'the tadpole philosophy, since the consolation it offers for social evils consists in the statement that exceptional individuals can succeed in evading them'. These exceptional individuals flourish, just as the best tadpoles become frogs, even though it is only by luck that they were born with or developed the appropriate qualities which most tadpoles lacked. The successful frogs may form the opinion that their success was justified, as the tadpoles had equal opportunities. That Tawney, like Cohen later, would accept a radical version of equality of opportunity but nothing less can be appreciated in the paragraph after his tadpole analogy:

> It is true, of course, that a community must draw on a stream of fresh talent, in order to avoid stagnation. ... But opportunities to rise are not a substitute for a large measure of practical equality, nor do they make immaterial the existence of sharp disparities of income and social condition. On the contrary, it is only the presence of a high degree of practical equality which can diffuse and generalize opportunities to rise. (Tawney, 1931: 143)

Many other British socialists, especially those of the Labour Party, have argued for a combination of liberty/freedom, equality and community, even though there has been no consensus on the meaning of those concepts or on how they should be ranked (Beech and Hickson, 2007: 3–6). In the early 1920s, for example, G.D.H. Cole, as an associationalist, perceived membership of groups and communities as crucial to human life. Community, he stressed in *Social Theory*, is 'a complex of social life' (Cole 1923: 25) more fundamental than society. The latter consists of organized associations and institutions to which a community gives rise. A community includes people who, in social relationships bound together by common but constantly changing customs, conventions and traditions, have conscious awareness of common goals and interests. Whilst being *connected* to associations formed for specific purposes, individuals *belong* to a community, which exists for the broader good life. Communities are elastic, their reality consisting in the consciousness of a changeable membership. 'Community' is thus a subjective term.

The internationalist aspect of Cole's socialism is evident in his suggestion that people could belong simultaneously to more than one community, each of which is 'an inclusive circle of social life'. 'Round many circles of family', he elaborated, 'may be drawn the wider circle of the city, and round many circles of city the yet wider circle of Province or the Nation, while round the circles of nation is drawn the yet wider and more cosmopolitan circle of world civilisation itself' (Cole, 1923: 26). The wider circles do not necessarily absorb the narrower ones within, each being an inclusive centre of life. The necessity to judge between conflicting loyalties demonstrates that fulfilling communal obligation requires cooperation. There was, for Cole (1923: 22), 'no such thing, strictly speaking, as the "will" of an association or institution; there are only the co-operating wills of its members'. He stressed, nevertheless, that structural principles make each social collective into 'something at least approaching a coherent whole' (Cole, 1923: 47–8). In the case of community, this principle is the sense of unity and social fellowship.

Turning to associations and institutions, Cole argued that the relevant principle for each is its function. Society – the complex of institutions and associations – is coherent when those entities perform their functions in a complementary manner necessary for social well-being. The development of a coherent society is thwarted and retarded insofar as the associations work either irrespective of their function in the social whole or according to purposes irreconcilable with the good of the whole (Cole, 1923: 50).

This distinctly socialist focus on the importance of community can be found as far back as in the works of Owen and Fourier. In 1808, in *The Theory of the Four Movements*, which is widely recognized, along with Owen's *A New View of Society*, as one of the key early socialist texts, Fourier (1996: 12) argued that an associative community could enable people to yield far more than a community of isolated families and thus provide them all with wealth and pleasure. Fourier devised a scheme for a series of groups. The groups would be formed by people to associate for functional reasons. According to Fourier (1996: 13), associative groups in the series would begin to cooperate in self-interest; but as the groups in the series encountered one another, they would recognize the tendency of human beings to seek concord and unity. He had, he believed, discovered the means to 'the most astounding, and happiest, event on this or any other globe, the transition from social chaos to universal harmony' (Fourier, 1996: 4).

As mentioned in the Introduction, *The Communist Manifesto* famously criticized thinkers such as Fourier and Owen for being Utopian. Before any realistic attempt to work for the good of all could take place, Marx and Engels (2002: 253–6) insisted, the existing society with its class divisions, inequalities and exploitation would need to be overthrown. Nevertheless, they considered community to be important in the future society, even though they rarely considered the details of such a society. As they put it in a well-known sentence which combines unstated concerns for equality and community with a clearly stated goal of freedom: 'In place of the old bourgeois society, with its classes and class antagonisms, we shall have an association, in which the free development of each is the condition for the free development of all' (Marx and Engels, 2000: 262). Until that time, the term 'community' had, they suggested in *The German Ideology* two years earlier, been applied to societies in which one class had combined against another, this therefore being a fetter upon the development of real communities. The earlier communities were thus illusory ones. 'In a real community', they went on, 'the individuals obtain their freedom in and through their association' (Marx and Engels, 1974: 83).

Marx thus had quite nuanced and complex views on equality. Later egalitarian theories, such as Cohen's, bear distinct affinities to those of Marx, even though Cohen (2000: 2–3) claimed that having in his youth and for some years after been a Marxist, he had become disillusioned with the ideology. To appreciate the complexity of Marx's view on equality, one should note his and Engels' rejection in *The Communist Manifesto* of the levelling down advocated by the early revolutionaries of the movement. Their literature, Marx and Engels suggested, had necessarily had a reactionary character. This was because the proletariat was in its undeveloped form and, in the absence of the advanced economic conditions which characterized modern capitalism and made emancipation possible, the result was 'universal ascetism and social levelling in its crudest form' (Marx and Engels, 2002: 253).

The profundity of Marx's thought on equality is also evident in his response to the Gotha programme. The programme was produced as part of a merger in 1875 between two rival German socialist parties: the Social Democratic Labour Party, which he and Engels supported, and the General German Workers' Association, inspired by the ideas of Marx's rival in the German socialist movement Ferdinand Lassalle (McLellan, 2006: 403–7; Sperber, 2013: 525–8). The programme presented largely Lassallean views.

Marx considered the Lassallean views on equality expressed in the Gotha programme to be too underdeveloped. 'From each according to his ability', Marx (1968b: 321) exclaimed in 1875 in his *Critique of the Gotha Programme*, 'to each according to his needs!' This egalitarian slogan, adopted from the French socialist Louis Blanc, is well known. One needs, however, to examine what Marx said in the surrounding text. One can thereby recognize a rather more nuanced argument for equality than might otherwise be appreciated. According to Marx, the Lassallean demand for equal rights whilst society is still dominated by the bourgeoisie – or in other words while society is still capitalist – was entirely inadequate and inappropriate. The problem was that 'the same principle prevails as in the exchange of commodity-equivalents: a given amount of labour in one form is exchanged for an equal amount of labour in another form' (Marx, 1968b; 319–20). Equal right would thus still in principle be bourgeois right, taking no consideration of difference. Marx was, however, acutely aware that society could not simply be reformed to make proper allowances for all such differences. As he put it: 'Right can never be higher than the economic structure of society and its cultural development conditioned thereby' (Marx, 1968b: 320). Hence, 'to each according to his needs' would need to be a longer-term goal, because to expect such rapid, fundamental change at once would be unrealistic. Society would still be conditioned in the short term by capitalist principles and theories. Such conditioning was what Marx had in mind sixteen years earlier when, in his 'Preface to *A Contribution to the Critique of Political Economy*', he wrote that relations of production correspond to the stage of development that productive forces have reached, and those relations of production constitute 'the real foundation, on which rises a legal and political superstructure and to which correspond definite forms of social consciousness' (Marx, 1968c: 181).

In the early 1930s, the innovative Marxist Antonio Gramsci, writing from the prison cell to which the Italian fascist regime had confined him, considered the means by which the consciousness of the masses was sometimes shaped without recourse to force or coercion. He offered a theory of hegemony as a form of dominance based on consent gained by shaping understandings and expectations about the nature of society, the naturalness of the existing economic relationships and the sort and extent of change or reform that can reasonably be demanded. The spontaneous consent of masses to the hegemony of each order is achieved due to 'the prestige (and consequent confidence) which the dominant group enjoys because of its position and function in the world of production' (Gramsci, 1971: 12).

Marx to some degree anticipated the problem of overcoming what Gramsci would refer to as hegemony. In *Critique of the Gotha Programme*, Marx advocated two phases of revolution. In the first, the bourgeois principle would be retained, and each would, equally, have a right to the equivalent of what they have produced. The aim would be to develop post-capitalist society into one which would enhance productive forces and individual capabilities. Importantly, culture, too, would change so that people would recognize the legitimacy of some fruits of their labour being available to those who were unable to produce as much as others. Hence, in the higher phase of communism, right would be unequal rather than equal. Marx's slogan demanding that each produces according to ability and takes what is needed for themselves and if necessary for their family would thus be acceptable according to the new culture.

In The *Communist Manifesto*, Marx and Engels advocated strict measures to be introduced temporarily by the communists upon seizing power to achieve social and economic conditions in which democracy would work for the working class. To appreciate this point, one must remember that political equality through extensions to the suffrage in capitalist societies had yet to be introduced. The first step of the working-class revolution was, Marx and Engels (2002: 243) declared, 'to raise the proletariat to the position of ruling class, to win the battle of democracy'. The existing socio-economic conditions and the assumptions about what was normal, possible and acceptable meant that even if political democratic arrangements were instituted, the working class would be able to achieve very little by means of them. Marx and Engels were concerned not only to introduce radical democracy, but also, as we saw in the sentence quoted earlier in the present chapter, to enable emancipated individuals to enjoy freedom for self-development in conjunction with all their fellows. A greater level of freedom could thereby be achieved than in the existing society, where people were concerned to compete with and exploit one another. This is what is known as a positive conception of freedom, as will become evident later in this chapter.

Marx thus had a sophisticated view of equality, democracy, freedom and the relationships between these three concepts. There is, furthermore, enough common ground in the views of Marx, Cohen and modern social democrats such as the British Labour Party theorist C.A.R. Crosland for them each to be categorized as socialist. In the 1950s, for example, Crosland (1956) argued that the egalitarian goal of social justice was to weaken the existing deep-seated class stratification of modern democracies such as Britain's, and that the process was already under way. As will be discussed in Chapters 4 and 5, a fundamental difference between Marx and Crosland was that the latter believed it possible for class-based exploitation to be eradicated, and substantial equality achieved, without radical action or political and social upheaval.

Broadening socialist equality

Whether or not radical action bringing political and social upheaval would be needed for the eradication of class-based exploitation, a question that has featured increasingly in debates on the left is whether socialists should look beyond such exploitation when considering how society needs to be changed. Turning again to Cohen, the implementation of his radical equality of opportunity would mean that some groups of people would almost certainly need to be treated very differently to narrow the gaps between their conditions and those of other members of society. This would be socialist equality, and it seems that Marx, judging from his statement about abilities and needs, would have concurred with Cohen. For both Marx and Cohen, the needs of all people should be catered for and each person would be given the opportunity to flourish in cooperation with, and without exploitation of, others. This may apply to disabled people, or to various other groups of people who suffer from discrimination, in which case there may be a need for some extra attention to aspects of society so that the practices and attitudes at issue can be removed, abolished or changed. Hence, whilst the narrowing of economic inequality of opportunity is central to socialist ideology, other sorts of inequality are also of concern, not least because they often relate to economic equality and exploitation directly or indirectly in various ways.

Building on their universalist principles, socialists began to develop views and debates on both sexual discrimination against women and other important issues, including racism and homophobia. Sometimes discrimination against certain groups means that members of them suffer economic inequality. They may be discouraged from taking certain jobs, for example, or their needs may not be met.

The case for the extension of socialist equality has been made succinctly by a number of thinkers in the USA. For Karen Brodkin Sacks in the late 1980s, the point was 'that one should not expect to find any generic worker or essential worker, or for that matter, working-class consciousness; that not only is class experienced in historically specific ways, but it is also experienced in racially specific, gender-specific, and kinship-specific ways' (Sacks, 1989: 542). The 'big issue', as she put it, was 'how to go about finding the unities and commonalities of class and class consciousness while being attentive to specificity' (Sacks, 1989: 543). Earlier that decade, the communist and feminist Angela Davis commented on the links between struggles against discrimination. Racism had, she claimed, 'always been used, in the first place, to pit workers against one another so that white workers can be led to believe that just because their skin is white like Mr Rockefeller's skin, they have more in common with their oppressors than they do with their Black or Chicano or Puerto Rican or Native American Indian sisters and brothers' (Davis, 1982: 8). Noting that affirmative action had first been employed to combat racism, she insisted the latter was 'something that it is absolutely necessary to eliminate if we are going to move on and achieve some of the victories that affect us as working-class people, as women, as disabled people, as lesbians and gay men' (Davis, 1982: 8). In 1952, in a largely ignored article titled 'Socialism and Sex', H.L. Small had argued that, as an important libertarian principle, legally of-age adults of both sexes should be free to have sexual relations with whomever they wish of the same or opposite sex, without fear of sanction. This would mean 'to the individual "deviant" that the fear of legal sanction, as well as illegal repression, blackmail, etc. are forever banished from his mind' (Small, in Phelps, 2007: 13).

Such freedom, Small continued, thus meant 'an area of operational freedom that will enable the emancipated individual to work and think more effectively in his tasks of everyday life'. As Christopher Phelps (2007: 12) suggests, Small was urging socialists to understand their commitment and goals in a sense that transcended narrow economic terms. Davis, Brodkin Sacks, Small and Phelps each help demonstrate why socialists and members of groups suffering discrimination should work cooperatively in the struggle for the collective greater good of their community and society.

The Marxist feminist Juliet Mitchell (1975) argued in the 1970s that working-class women need to engage in a dual struggle. First, in the class struggle against capitalist exploitation, they and men should work alongside one another. Second, women need to work within their own political movement against exploitation in their work at home. Work at home reduces and cheapens the labour power that women can sell. Such work is useful to capitalism in two ways. First, although not of market value as it does not produce things that can be exchanged for goods or services of equivalent worth, it provides the conditions whereby men of this and future generations can work in the capitalist economy.

Second, Mitchell noted, the indispensable role of women as consumers appears natural, disguising and legitimating the capitalist system it underpins.

Also in the 1970s, Sheila Rowbotham (2013: 178–82, 194–201, 208–34) argued that socialists should encourage the open expression of difference in order to challenge discrimination. If connections were made with the different groups which faced discrimination, this would help bring them into the socialist fold. The ideological overlapping of socialism and feminism is thus evident in her argument. Rowbotham challenged the authoritarian and hierarchical principles of Leninism as incompatible with the socialist-feminist rejection of hierarchy. Capitalism, she argues, exploits not just the traditional working class, but also a range of other groups whose identities and problems should be recognized. The focus on groups retains the sociality of socialism. A coalition of such groups, including the working class, is needed as a means of challenging corporate capitalism, presently legitimized by an individualist doctrine. Socialists and feminists need to work together to either overcome or considerably temper capitalist exploitation while communitarian fellowship is achieved.

Like Rowbotham, Ernesto Laclau and Chantal Mouffe sought to combine the struggle of the working class with that of other groups against capitalism. Although the importance of strategy for socialism was prominent in the title of their influential 1985 book *Hegemony and Socialist Strategy*, Laclau and Mouffe believed that socialists should recognize the need to combine with other movements fighting oppression in contemporary capitalist society, without assuming that socialism should hold precedence. Unlike Rowbotham, Laclau and Mouffe were not concerned with persuading members of the other groups to be socialists. Every project for radical democracy, they insisted, 'implies a socialist dimension, as it is necessary to put an end to capitalist relations of production, which are at the root of numerous relations of subordination; but socialism is *one* of the components of a project for radical democracy, not vice versa' (Laclau and Mouffe, 1985: 178). Anticolonial, antiracist, environmentalist, gay and lesbian movements highlighted equally significant forms of oppression. It was necessary for such movements to work together in opposition to the existing hegemonic power which underpinned capitalist dominance. The opposition required counter-hegemony to be built and articulated by the various groups in an emancipatory discourse combination which would expand and secure the chains of equivalence that could hold together various struggles against oppression (Laclau and Mouffe, 1985: 159–71). In the struggle against the existing hegemony, socialists would have to accept that identity and culture were equally as significant as class.

Some socialist feminists, such as the German Marxist Clara Zetkin in 1903, have warned against placing too great an emphasis on the exploitation of women in general, arguing that this serves to hide the vast inequalities between bourgeois women and working-class women. For a socialist society to be achieved, it was, according to Zetkin, important that the proletariat, especially proletarian women, conquered political power. This, she suggested, was 'the painful path of the development that leads the female sex from social servitude to freedom' (Zetkin, 1990: 240).

Compared to Zetkin, Nancy Fraser (1995) took a far more complex approach. Arguing that the attention taken away from class and capitalist exploitation by emphasis upon identity and culture was problematical, Fraser acknowledged that there are genuine problems to be resolved in each field. She drew attention to cases where a person may simultaneously experience economic exploitation and discrimination on grounds of race or gender. A transformative solution would, she argued, combine the introduction of socialist measures in the economy and politics with a deconstructive resolution of cultural dichotomies. The binary oppositions would be revealed as false and thus cultural equality would be encouraged to grow. Around a decade earlier, at the time of Margaret Thatcher's conservative governments in the UK, in a volume recommending how the Labour Party should build a democratic socialist society once it returned to power, Jane Lewis (1983: 120) advocated a shift in thinking towards the 'pursuit of substantive rather than formal sex equality'. This would involve the redefinition of work within the family and the workplace, calling into question the legitimation of sex equality.

Far more diverse, nuanced and sophisticated than the crude levelling with which it is sometimes associated, socialism is also more complex than suggested by Newman's claim that equality is *the* most fundamental characteristic. Freedom is equally important to socialists, notwithstanding considerable disagreement regarding what such freedom involves. As Axel Honneth (2017: 6–26) makes clear, the belief that freedom can best be achieved in solidarity and cooperation with other members of the community has been a key aspect of socialist thought from the very beginning of the movement. The influence of the eighteenth-century philosopher Jean-Jacques Rousseau is significant in this respect.

The influence of Rousseau

According to Bernard Crick (1987: 10), Rousseau was the idealizer of the common man. This common man was the peasant, craftsman or small shopkeeper rather than the modern working-class person of the industrial revolution. Rousseau had not denounced class or property *per se*, but only their abuse through pride, luxury and power. The 'moral attributes of [Rousseau's] somewhat rural, certainly pre-industrial, common man could', Crick (1987: 10) suggested, nevertheless 'easily be transferred to the class-conscious urban workingman'.

By no means all socialists acknowledge or recognize Rousseau's significance. His combination of egalitarian, communitarian and libertarian ideas did, however, help shape the milieu in which dissatisfaction with the conditions of capitalist society was channelled. Important in this respect were Rousseau's 'Discourse on the Origin of Inequality' and *The Social Contract*.

In his 'Discourse', from 1755, Rousseau exclaimed that modern society and law came into being when ordinary people 'all ran headlong to their chains, in hopes of securing their liberty'. This, in turn, 'bound new fetters on the poor, and gave new powers to the rich; which irretrievably destroyed natural liberty, eternally fixed the law of property and equality ... and, for the advantage of a few ambitious individuals, subjected all mankind to perpetual labour, slavery, and wretchedness' (Rousseau, 1993a: 99). Fourier (1996: 281) applauded Rousseau's view of civilization as 'an inversion of nature's wishes, a systematic development of all the vices'. In *The Communist Manifesto*, Marx and Engels (2002: 253–6) criticized Fourier for his inability to recognize the necessity for proletarian (working-class) revolution, but admired his criticism of capitalism (Beecher, 2019: 219, 226). Rousseau's influence thus reached them at least in part via Fourier. Although reluctant to praise Rousseau, Marx drew on his ideas in 1875. Criticizing the vagueness of the Gotha Programme's statement that no 'useful' labour was possible outside society, Marx (1968b: 316) added that only in society could 'useless and even harmful labour become a branch of gainful occupation ... in short, one could just as well have copied the whole of Rousseau'. What socialists needed to do, Marx insisted, was to prove that material conditions had already developed which 'enable and compel the workers to lift this social curse'. Workers would thus emancipate themselves.

In *The Social Contract*, from 1762, Rousseau presented his theory of the general will, which is what people would will if they were aware that their best interests, like those of others collectively in their community, coincided with the common good. Rousseau argued that people could realize autonomy (meaning self-rule) and thus freedom in this way (Rousseau, 1993b) and that they may need to be forced to be free, meaning they would be compelled to accept that it is in their best interests. Whilst perhaps rhetorical, this forcing of freedom has authoritarian and even totalitarian connotations unacceptable to many socialists. Nevertheless, the notion of recognizing that our best interests are shared in common struck a chord. Cole, for example, sought to find a less authoritarian way for people to achieve autonomy through the general will (Lamb, 2005).

Cole argued (1914–15: 149–50) in his paper 'Conflicting Social Obligations' that 'the key to any rational social theory must be found in some conception of a General Will'. This collective will is generated when each person disregards the individual aspect of their will and thinks in terms of the social aspect of that will. Social organization, or 'social machinery', is, for Cole (1914–15: 141), 'the organisation of human will'. In cases of conflict, social obligation is owed to the machinery that, as an instrument of cooperative action, best serves the whole community.

In his paper 'Loyalties' eleven years later, Cole conceded that his focus on obligation rather than loyalty had overemphasized the duties of individuals, giving inadequate consideration to sociality. Sociality was the part of natural will that was expressed in cooperative relations between humans in their associations. 'Loyalty' meant 'that common sentiment of us all which is the whole basis of our capacity to live and work together' (Cole, 1925–6: 154–5). People were capable of willing universally, and this required harmony, which in turn needed 'at least the broad conception of a common plan' (Cole, 1925–6: 162). For the social to flourish, the anti-social motives of individuals needed to be overcome. This would necessitate the harmony of society's institutions with the best use of material resources to enable people to assert their power over nature (Cole, 1925–6: 169). Sociality, which was natural for human beings, thus needed to be fostered. This emphasis on sociality created by individual human relations exemplifies the socialist view that an environment can be created wherein people could achieve flourishing unachievable by individuals acting alone. Social freedom would thus be compatible with fraternity, solidarity and equality.

In socialist societies which do not suppress opposing ideas, the authorities may face challenges. In this case, the attempt to combine equality and freedom may fail (Connolly, 1977). Education and socialization may produce a situation where most people agree that social freedom is more important than the negative freedom to do whatever one wants to, freedom thus being compatible with equality. Nevertheless, the minority who resist would still have a point. Socialist equality and socialist freedom or liberty would involve what has come to be known as luck egalitarianism. The unfortunate in terms of skills, knowledge, energy, stamina, inventiveness, enterprise, and so on, would be compensated, which would involve restrictions on what the fortunate could achieve individually. Taxation, for example, would involve effort-harnessing – the effort of the fortunate thus helping the less fortunate along (White, 2007: 91–2). While there may be strong moral arguments for effort-harnessing, it does pose a problem: the previously fortunate may suggest that according to their preferred interpretation of freedom they suffer encroachments in the interests of equality.

Socialists must therefore find a way to justify their position, and there are various, often competing, meanings of equality and freedom on which they might draw. An important distinction tends to be drawn between negative and positive conceptions of freedom or liberty – a distinction often interpreted as one between freedom from restraint and freedom to do something. This, however, is unhelpful, for two reasons. First, any freedom from restraint is also a freedom to do something, and vice versa, even if either from or to is unstated or elliptical. Second, the distinction sows confusion owing to further differing interpretations which conceive of the positive in different ways. Such interpretations include (a) that which distinguishes between formal freedom (absence of interference) and effective freedom (having the capacity and/ or power to do something, and (b) that which considers the distinction to be between doing what one wants and having autonomy (Swift, 2001: 51–64). The latter can become the basis of authoritarianism or even totalitarianism when accompanied by an argument that some people (perhaps those in a particular party) are able to guide others into autonomy by recommending certain ideas and discouraging others. This further division of the negative and positive binary opposition will not help us elaborate on the interpretation of socialist freedom, which, as we saw earlier in this chapter, one can find in Honneth's study. The division can, however, help clarify what particular socialists are proposing and whether their arguments are convincing.

Positive and negative freedom in socialist theory

An early example of emancipatory theory in terms of positive freedom can be found in *The Communist Manifesto*, in which Marx and Engels insisted that the class division and class antagonisms of bourgeois society would be replaced by a communist society wherein people would collectively enjoy free development. In terms of autonomy, Marx and Engels seem to have believed that the Communist Party would have an educational role in helping people attain that condition. The positive libertarian aspect of the socialist tradition, in which Marx and Engels were thus significant, has been interpreted in authoritarian terms by some later Marxist-Leninist theorists. This, once again, can be seen as a strategy for emancipation in terms of both effective freedom and autonomy. Of course, one may argue that seeking to gain the sort of effective freedom and/or autonomy deemed achievable is not a worthwhile pursuit if the extent of restrictions on doing what one wants to, and thus the interference in one's life, is excessive. An example that illustrates the extreme authoritarian and even totalitarian uses to which the positive conception of freedom can be put can be found in Joseph Stalin's writings of the 1920s. First, however, one of Marx's key terms needs to be introduced.

In *Critique of the Gotha Programme*, Marx (1968b: 327) used the term 'revolutionary dictatorship of the proletariat'. To interpret this as a blunt call for an oppressive dictatorship, however, would be to miss the point he was making. The argument for dictatorship would seem incompatible with the views he expressed about equality in the same document and indeed with his views on freedom in works such as *The Communist Manifesto*. Marx insisted that this must be for a transitional period before the introduction of the higher phase of communism in a society. The dictatorship of the proletariat was therefore not intended as a permanent arrangement for an advanced society. Dictatorship, moreover, did not have the very authoritarian connotations associated with it by the twentieth century. Consistently with its original usage in ancient republican Rome, 'dictatorship' in Marx's time signified a short transitional arrangement granted to the ruler to defend the republic (Fraser and Wilde, 2011: 78). Measures would be firm and authoritarian but not necessarily as suppressive and despotic as the term has come to signify today.

Stalin took Marx's rather vague notion of the dictatorship of the proletariat and interpreted it literally as a dictatorship in the modern sense of the term: an uncompromising, authoritarian form of leadership; in this case it was such leadership by the vanguard of the Soviet Communist Party. The important implications for freedom can be appreciated by first noting Stalin's description of the dictatorship of the proletariat as a 'guiding force' in terms of its structure, mechanism and function, which he portrayed graphically as a system of belts and levers. 'The proletariat', he argued, 'needs these belts, these levers, and this guiding force, because without them it would, in its struggle for victory, be like a weaponless army in face of organised and armed capital' (Stalin, 1928: 29). This raises the question of who or what provides the guidance. Stalin (1928: 418) provides the following answer: 'The importance of the Party as the guiding energy in all these things is immeasurable. The dictatorship of the proletariat does not run itself; it can only work thanks to the forces of the Party and under the guidance of the Party.'

According to Stalin (1928: 110), the dictatorship of the proletariat was 'the chief fulcrum of the proletarian revolution, its main instrument', the first aim of which was 'to break the resistance of the defeated exploiters'. While this authoritarian and uncompromising aim is not yet being portrayed as freedom, what for Stalin would be the next act of the dictatorship is significant. The dictatorship must, he insisted, 'lead the revolution onward to the final victory, to the complete triumph of socialism' (Stalin, 1928: 110). The significance becomes clear in the following words: 'Only under the dictatorship of the proletariat can there be real freedom for the exploited masses, and only under the dictatorship of the proletariat can the workers and the peasants effectively participate in the government of the country' (Stalin, 1928: 116). A new form of state organization would bring the 'full liberation' of the 'labouring masses' from 'every form of oppression and exploitation' (Stalin, 1928: 119). The rights of the exploiting minority would be restricted while theoretically the proletariat and exploited peasants gain effective freedom in the positive sense. The Soviet power would unite the executive and legislative authority into a single organ which would be 'the embodiment of a majoritarian dictatorship' (Stalin, 1928: 120).

Intuitively, it seems that, even if Stalin's socialist freedom may be acceptable in the short term to people who have faced severe hardship under previous regimes, dissatisfaction with harsh dictatorship would begin to grow. The revolutions that erupted in Eastern Europe in 1989 help substantiate this intuition, as does the protest in Tiananmen Square, China, that year. Hard-line Stalinists may argue that this is all the work of Western influences corrupting the minds of citizens in socialist societies. There are, however, too many examples of rebellion against authoritarian socialist rule for those arguments to ring true. Hence, for a more acceptable form of socialist freedom one, must look elsewhere.

Julius Nyerere's African socialist project gets us little further. With Nyerere as prime minister, Tanganyika gained independence from the UK in 1961. He became president the following year and in 1964 the country was renamed Tanzania. For the next twenty years, Nyerere presided over an attempt to build a society combining core tenets of socialism with traditional African values. A socialist vision of freedom was a core feature of the project. As he put it in his article 'From Uhuru to Ujamaa' (from freedom to socialism), he and his colleagues in the Tanganyika African National Union (TANU) had been 'trying to create a society in which all citizens work together in freedom, dignity and equality, for their common good' (Nyerere, 1974: 8). Important objectives included freedom from racist rule, economic domination, poverty, injustice, oppression and mental subjugation to ideas which emanated from the West. This goal thus involved a significant negative element of freedom from restraint. However, if one looks closely at Nyerere's account of difficulties encountered and mistakes made in the project, there is also a crucial positive element.

Nyerere's government introduced a one-party system in 1965. People were, as he put it, 'able to choose between different TANU Parliamentary candidates and thus express their opinions about individuals without casting doubt upon their loyalty to TANU' (Nyerere, 1974: 5). Whilst significant progress was made in the first few years of the new political system, he conceded 'that the socialism we claimed to support was not being reflected in consistent domestic policies'. The problem was that 'our policies were leading to the development of individualistic attitudes and aspira-tions by political leaders and by the newly educated young people' (Nyerere, 1974: 6). Socialism, according to TANU's Arusha declaration of 1967, would involve self-reliance and active democracy. Nyerere conceded that in 1974 continuing poverty, inequality, malnutrition and lack of education meant that Tanzania had yet to become a socialist country. Nevertheless, he insisted, he and his party were still building socialism by 'creating a society which is based on cooper-ation and which excludes the exploitation of man by man'. People were 'working together in cooperative production for their common benefit' (Nyerere, 1974: 7).

The ruling party in the one-party system was, for Nyerere, operating democratically, albeit not according to the Western form of democracy. As he had put in an article of 1961 making the case for one-party rule, traditionally, African tribal societies – even those with chiefs – were societies of equals conducting their business by way of discussion. This African form of democracy did not need competing parties. Furthermore, Tanzania, like other new African societies upon independence, was in a condition of emergency, and it had to be remembered that in Western democracies parties had sunk their differences to form national governments not unlike the one-party rule he was advocating. It was the responsibility of government in a democratic country to lead the fight against enemies of freedom. 'To do this', he claimed, 'the government, once freely elected, must also be free to govern in the best interests of the people, and without fear of sabotage' (Nyerere, 1997: 159). One can assume that Nyerere believed that a choice of TANU candidates would ensure that electors would receive suitable guidance on how to achieve autonomy. Nyerere's was thus a positive conception of freedom in terms of both efficiency and autonomy. It was authoritarian but less overtly confronta-tional with opponents than that of Stalin – or perhaps Stalin was simply less dishonest regarding suppression.

A less authoritarian positive interpretation of freedom can be found in the British Labour Party thinker Harold Laski's *A Grammar of Politics*. Liberty, he suggested, 'is a positive thing' which 'does not merely mean absence of restraint'. 'Liberty' meant 'the eager maintenance of that atmosphere in which men have the opportunity to be their best selves' and 'best self' meant 'the full development of our faculties' (Laski, 1925: 142). A state built on conditions essential to such development would 'confer freedom on its citizens', enabling them 'to contribute their peculiar and intimate experience to the common stock'. This was thus positive freedom in terms of both autonomy and effectiveness.

There is no dictatorial guidance in Laski's version of positive freedom. 'Liberty', he stated, 'is not merely obedience to a rule.' Each person's self was too distinct from other selves for liberty to be reduced as such. Whilst insisting there must be common rules and restrictions, he elaborated as follows:

> It is ... essential to freedom that the prohibitions issued should be built upon the wills of those whom they affect. I must be able to feel that my will has access to avenues through which it can impress itself upon the holders of power. If I have the sense that the orders issued are beyond my scrutiny or criticism, I shall be, in a vital sense, unfree. (Laski, 1925: 143)

Although thus interpreting freedom in terms of will, Laski rejected the coercive aspect of Rousseau's theory because it advocated 'a kind of permanent tutelage to the real self embodied in the State', whereby freedom would be 'suffused with the sense of compulsion'. This, for Laski (1925: 30–1), would amount to the 'paralysis of will'.

The non-authoritarian nature of Laski's theory of freedom was substantiated when, in *Liberty in the Modern State*, he offered a definition he portrayed as negative, even though it differed little in substance from his earlier positive theory. By 'liberty' he now meant 'the absence of restraint upon the existence of those social conditions which, in modern civilization, are the necessary guarantees of individual happiness' (Laski, 1930: 11). In what may appear as a clean break from his earlier theory, he stressed that he was maintaining a thesis that 'liberty is essentially an absence of restraint', implying 'power to expand, the choice by the individual of his own way of life without imposed prohibitions from without' (Laski, 1930: 11). Rousseau was thus wrong, he went on, to say people could 'be forced into freedom'. 'By making liberty the absence of restraint,' Laski (1930: 12–13) confirmed, 'I make it, of course, a purely negative condition.'

Laski had come to think in terms of a particular sort of negative freedom. A person deprived of security in employment, he suggested, 'becomes the prey of a mental and physical servitude incompatible with the very essence of freedom'. Although, he went on, economic security was not liberty, it was 'a condition without which liberty is never effective' (Laski, 1930: 13). Similarly, deprivation of knowledge was 'not a denial of liberty' but, rather, 'a denial of the power to use liberty for great ends'. This would make somebody, 'inevitably, the slave of those more fortunate than himself' (Laski, 1930: 14).

His prose seemingly tying itself in knots, Laski was seeking a negative conception of social freedom: distinguishing single instances of freedom from that which requires absence of constraint upon self-development. Perhaps he should have reformulated his earlier positive conception rather than try to work with the negative. However, one can appreciate his efforts when his motive for abandoning the positive is taken into consideration: he had been alarmed by first-hand reports about the manipulation of the positive conception in Italy. The fascist ruler Benito Mussolini and his loyal philosopher Giovanni Gentile were legitimating policy and action which forced people to accept what was ostensibly freedom (Lamb, 2004: 79).

The compatibility of liberty and equality is an issue many other socialists have sought to address. They each in their different ways argue that an egalitarian society could be one where each person enjoys freedom or liberty from exploitation in fellowship with others, and thus achieves self-development. Theory which does not include such a combination even indirectly is usually either clearly recognizable as falling outside the socialist camp or, where the theory offers a masquerade that succeeds in gaining a following, brings both itself and socialism in general into disrepute – the obvious example being the national socialism of Adolf Hitler's Germany. Nazism did not bring about anything like the combination of freedom and equality that lies at the core of socialism. Theories intending to justify fascist practice in such terms were based on myths to mobilize the people and arguments to justify hierarchy, superiority and the need to suppress, which had no place in socialism. Some former socialists such as Robert Michels, Henri de Man and Oswald Mosely produced an ideological variant – referred to by Zeev Sternhell (1979: 371–9) as neo-socialism – which sought to justify fascism and Nazism as the means to counter capitalist power. Such opposition to capitalism was, however, partial; like other fascist movements and regimes, Nazism opposed financial capital but collaborated with other large-scale sectors of capitalism (Neocleous, 1997: 39–58). Hence, the ostensive ideological overlap is unsubstantiated and the use of the word 'socialist' in national socialism inappropriate. Of course, Marxism-Leninism under Stalin was equally brutal and authoritarian; but the arguments presented in its justification are ones of brutal and authoritarian socialism, however uncomfortable other socialists feel about this.

Turning from one socialist extreme to another, Labour Party leader Tony Blair's social-ism avoided direct reference to freedom or liberty. Envisaging cooperation between classes, Blair was to many socialists wildly optimistic; but socialist principles are recognizable in his view of sociality, his notions of equality and community and his ideas of overcoming capitalist domination ethically by means of persuading capitalists. The left, he insisted, should intervene with policies that will 'equip and advance the individual's ability to prosper within [the] new economy' (Blair, 1994: 5). Perhaps Blair was wise to avoid the intellectual contortions of the positive–negative freedom distinction. Without direct reference to the emancipatory objective, however, socialism risks losing both its identity and an understanding of the magnitude of the obstacles which capitalism places in the path of that objective. The next chapter will consider socialist views on the state in terms of, on the one hand, a means but, on the other hand, obstacles to that objective.

3
The State and the Economy

Socialists differ in their views on what should be done about the existing state operating within the capitalist economic system. Some argue that, tied as it is to the property system, the capitalist state must be demolished and replaced by one which genuinely represents working people. Marxist-Leninists in power have argued that their new state does this and is in the course of building the socialist society. Other socialists insist that the existing state can be either captured as a means of introducing a collective property system or, less radically, employed to regulate property ownership. Then there are socialists who seek in various ways to transfer considerable power from the existing state to associations and to organize society, its economy and thus the property system accordingly. Whether a reformed state or a new one designed for socialist purposes is sought, a related question concerns the requisite extent of intervention by that state in the economy.

As they consider these issues, socialists seek, in various ways, to regulate or abolish private property insofar as it thwarts a reasonable standard of life for ordinary people and prevents those people from achieving social freedom. One thing upon which socialists agree is that a socialist economy cannot keep the capitalist property system unchanged. This chapter will examine these matters of agreement and disagreement, leading to the discussion in Chapter 4 of socialist views on how to bring about social and political change.

The nature of the state

A well-known line in Marx and Engels' *Communist Manifesto* is traditionally translated from German to English as follows: 'The executive of the modern State is but a committee for managing the common affairs of the whole bourgeoisie' (Marx and Engels, 2002: 221). There is, however, some disagreement regarding the wording of the sentence (Lamb, 2015: 34–5). Terrell Carver's translation mentions neither an executive nor a committee, instead rendering the same sentence as: 'The power of the state is merely a device for administrating the common affairs of the whole bourgeoisie' (Marx and Engels, 1996: 3). However, what is crucial is that these translations each illustrate Marx and Engels' point that the state represents the broader interests of the whole bourgeoisie, notwithstanding divisions within that class on narrower concerns. Each translation is, indeed, consistent with Marx's argument in 1859 that a political and legal superstructure both builds on and reflects the economic structure of society (Marx, 1968c: 181).

The *Manifesto* was published during the period of failed revolutions in Paris and several other European capitals in 1848. Marx offered similar views regarding the power of the state and the common affairs of the bourgeoisie in *The Eighteenth Brumaire of Louis Bonaparte*, in which he discussed the events which led the various factions of the French bourgeoisie to accept the seizure of power by Louis-Napoleon in 1851 and to tolerate his autocratic rule. (The title of the work plays on the fact that in 1799 Louis-Napoleon's uncle, Napoleon Bonaparte, had seized power in the month of Brumaire in the republican calendar.) Marx (1968d) argued that while the bourgeoisie was divided, the different divisions shared interests that the state upholds by maintaining order. He was thus discussing what later came to be known as the relative autonomy of the state.

A different interpretation of the nature of the state was expressed by Marx's rival Ferdinand Lassalle in an open letter to the National Labour Association of Germany in 1863. Through parliamentary action, Lassalle insisted, the working class could, fundamentally, reform the existing state into an organization to serve the interests of that class. Lassalle argued that the state could, consequently, enable the working class to take control of their factories and industries. Although some groups of workers, especially in England, had achieved some betterment of conditions, 'there remains to be accomplished the real improvement of the condition of labor embracing the entire class, and which can only be done through help advanced by the state' (Lassalle, 1990: 91). It was, moreover, the duty of the state to do so. In fact, the state's mission was 'to expedite and assure the advance of culture' (Lassalle, 1990: 92), and the 'elevation of the working class ought to be regarded as the grandest achievement of culture, therefore warranting the highest efforts of the state in the accomplishment' (Lassalle, 1990: 93). After all, the state comprised the consolidated people. Remember this, he advised the working class: 'you, the people, are the state' (Lassalle, 1990: 96).

Lassalle argued that the credit necessary to implement a plan for control by workers of their industries would be procured by means of the state for the 'association of the entire working class'. This could only happen gradually. 'As soon as a number of such associations would be formed,' he argued, 'securing the aid of the state, their existence would make it easier to introduce them to other branches of industry, which, when combined, would form a chain of credit with relation to one another' (Lassalle, 1990: 94). An insurance association would be founded, paying weekly wages to workers and distributing business profits to them in the form of dividends.

Unlike Lassalle, Marxists argue that the existing state, and any other that follows it without abolishing the wage system, works primarily for the dominant capitalist class. Marx and Lassalle each recognized progress in terms of increased productivity. While the workers may receive some benefits from this increase, Lassalle (1990: 86–7) argued, again thus far consistently with Marx, the dominant classes would receive more. Marx, however, identified a key weakness in this aspect of Lassallean theory. Even if the workers were to begin to enjoy substantial and consistent improvements in their lives, Lassalle (1990: 89) suggested, wages would fall. He described this as 'a merciless economic rule' guided by the 'so-called law of supply and demand' (Lassalle, 1990: 84–5), in obedience to which average wages always remain reduced to a rate not far above that needed for existence and propagation. Whilst for Lassalle, however, it was thus not at present of real value to the working class, the state in his view did not *necessarily* act in the interests of the dominant class.

Drawing on Lassalle's idea of the 'merciless economic rule', twelve years later the Gotha Programme called for the abolition of the wage system together with the 'iron law of wages' (McLellan, 2006: 403). In his critical response, Marx cited and exposed the weakness of the passage in the Programme which said a socialist society would need to abolish this 'law' and the exploitation it brought about. Even if there is such a thing as the 'iron law of wages', Marx (1968b: 324) protested, 'I *cannot* abolish the law even if I abolish wage labour a hundred times over, because the law then governs not only the system of wage labour but *every* social system.' For Marx, as there was no such law, the capitalist social system could not thereby be replaced by a classless social system, exploitation by the dominant class would remain and, owing to increased productivity, be proportionately greater 'whether the worker receives better or worse payment' (Marx, 1968b: 325). So, for Marx, not only were the Lassalleans talking nonsense, but the point was to change the social system rather than the state.

Marxists after Marx have likewise analysed the working of the capitalist state and its role in the capitalist economic system. Antonio Gramsci argued in the 1920s and 1930s that the state protected the interests of the dominant class by means of hegemony rather than simply coercion. As hegemony thus brought legitimacy, the state did not need constant, conscious and direct interference from the dominant class to ensure it worked in favour of the vested interests. Hegemony, moreover, according to Gramsci (1971: 247, 260), involved the state as educator and as an instrument of rationalization, by which he meant routine use of procedures which normalize domination. Because it reflected civil society (by which he meant the complex structure of private relations including the economy), the state was insulated from challenges to its authority. As he put it:

> The superstructures of civil society are like the trench-systems of modern warfare. In war it would sometimes happen that a fierce artillery attack seemed to have destroyed the enemy's entire defensive system, whereas in fact it had only destroyed the outer perimeter; and at the moment of their advance and attack the assailants would find themselves confronted by a line of defence which was still effective. The same thing happens in politics, during the great economic crises. (Gramsci, 1971: 235)

Later in the century, Marxists discussed the related issue of relative autonomy, meaning that the state is not simply an instrument of the dominant class. As long as it did not present a fundamental challenge to the economic system, the state could make laws, policies and decisions favouring other classes. In the late 1960s and early 1970s, Ralph Miliband and Nicos Poulantzas debated the reasons why this was possible.

In 1968, Poulantzas offered a structural explanation in *Pouvoir politique et classes sociales*, translated into English as *Political Power and Social Classes* in 1973. The capitalist mode of production, he argued, consisted of an ensemble of structures operating in the different economic, political, military, cultural and other fields, and at different levels of them. These fields were relatively autonomous vis-à-vis one another and from the state. The capitalist state was thus relatively autonomous vis-à-vis the classes and factions, along with their allies, which operated within this ensemble. While ostensibly neutral, functioning as a factor of unity, the state ultimately, however, defended the stronger classes and factions (Poulantzas, 1973: 115, 255–7), not least by presenting a picture of general interest reflected in political democracy and popular sovereignty (Poulantzas, 1973: 124, 277–8).

Miliband sought instead to explain the role of the state in capitalist countries in terms of relationships between the dominant class, the state institutions which that class largely controlled and elected governments. He argued in *The State in Capitalist Society* that progress in terms of democracy, equality and social mobility had not significantly reduced the domination of the political, legal and military systems by people of privileged class background. (Miliband, 1969: 66–7). In response, Poulantzas (1969: 69–70, 73) argued that in claiming that the elite was dominated by the capitalist class, Miliband inadvertently drew attention away from the role of the entire capitalist system, and the state's function within it, in maintaining capitalist class dominance.

Miliband (1983: 31) did sometimes mention 'the structural constraints of the system', and Poulantzas (1973: 23) did, however briefly, acknowledge that the workings of actual capitalist states were significant. The disagreement between them boils down to one of emphasis. Poulantzas considered abstract theory more important while Miliband focused closely on who was performing what role, and with what influence, in capitalist states. Insisting that empirical inquiry was equally as important as presenting an alternative theory to that being opposed, Miliband (1983: 29) suggested that the best way to attack bourgeois theory was to turn the concept of elite 'against those who use it for apologetic purposes'.

Later in the 1970s, Fred Block (1977) offered a structural explanation which incorporated a key aspect of Miliband's work. Because of the necessity to maintain business confidence, especially in an international capitalist system wherein business can easily exit a particular country, Block argued, a government needs to maintain conditions conducive to investment. This is necessary for the regime in question to secure stability in the economy, this being a condition of its electoral fortunes. Like Poulantzas, Block saw this as a structural mechanism, state managers being forced by their structural position to become conscious of ways in which they can apply influence and thereby maintain the viability of the social order. Block acknowledged that the consciousness of the managers is instilled in part by the conscious activity of members of the ruling class, but considered this to be of secondary importance. As he put it:

The influence channels make it less likely that state managers will formulate policies that conflict directly with the interests of capitalists. But it is a subsidiary mechanism because even in the absence of these influence channels, other structural mechanisms make it extremely difficult for the state managers to carry through anti-capitalist policies. (Block, 1977: 14)

Considered together, the theories of Miliband, Poulantzas and Block help show that policies which oppose capitalism at what Martin Seliger (1976: 175) called the operational level of ideology would need to address the very function of capitalism, both as a structural system and as a set of institutions populated by human beings.

Poulantzas' account of property in his structural theory in fact links structure to humans in the institutions of capitalism. For him, capitalism is 'a relation of property' in that 'it makes the non-labourer intervene as owner either of the means of production or of labour-power or both, and so of the product' (Poulantzas, 1973: 26). This property relation defined the relations of production. Poulantzas thus expressed the tendency for socialists to see the function of capitalism in terms of the defence of an inequitable distribution of property which the capitalist state manages and defends.

The state and the issue of property ownership

All socialists need to address the implications and consequences of property rights in capitalist society and the role of the state in that respect. Otherwise, their contribution, whether theoretical or practical, will miss the point of the movement, which is to replace the existing exploitative society with one arranged on a communal, egalitarian basis for social freedom, in which humans flourish. The adjective 'social' here is important. When they consider the issue of property, socialists must impose restraints on the possessive individualist type of freedom if equality, community and human flourishing are to be realized. G.A. Cohen (2009: 1–45) sought to illustrate the importance of equality, community and flourishing in an imaginary 'camping trip' example. When the campers acted on the basis of equality moderated by community, the camp was efficient and enjoyable. When they began to think in terms of property, it deteriorated. Society, he argued, could, with suitable organizational technology, similarly operate better on socialist principles (Cohen 2009: 57–8).

A key question for socialists is whether the issues of property can be resolved without resort to a revolutionary break from capitalism. Eduard Bernstein (1993: 102) suggested that, although they had usually considered the revolutionary path to be 'inevitable, nearly everywhere', late in life Marx and Engels might have sympathized with the transformation of social democracy from a revolutionary to a parliamentary form of socialism in the changing circumstances. Perhaps Bernstein had in mind a period in the 1860s when Marx had worked closely with English trade unionists in their attempts to gain reform by means of universal suffrage (Stedman Jones, 2017: 470–5). However, by the early 1870s, Marx was clearly supporting revolutionary action again, such as his defence of the Paris Commune, whereby, at the end of the Franco-Prussian War of 1870–1, citizens of the French capital temporarily took control of the city until this endeavour was crushed by the authorities (Stedman Jones, 2017: 494–510). In *The Civil War in France*, he offered a report and interpretation of the Commune (Marx, 1968e). In general, Marx and Marxists have tended to be sceptical of the prospects for parliamentary attempts to bear fruit, believing the dominant class will only tolerate regulation until it encroaches significantly on property rights and holdings. The issue of revolutionary or parliamentary roads to socialism is discussed in the next chapter. Here, we are concerned with the problem of property that generates the issue.

In the first volume of *Capital*, Marx was clear that the reluctance to regulate was deeply ingrained in the capitalist system. As he put it:

> The same bourgeois consciousness which celebrates the division of labour in the workshop, the lifelong annexation of the labourer to a partial operation, and his complete

subjection to capital, as an organization of labour that increases its productive power, denounces with equal vigour every conscious attempt to control and regulate the process of production socially, as an inroad upon such sacred things as the rights of property, freedom and the self-determining 'genius' of the individual capitalist. (Marx, 1976: 477)

This passage helps illustrate more fully what Marx and Engels meant in the famous statement of *The Communist Manifesto* about the state managing or administering the common affairs of the bourgeoisie. Such management or administration would not extend to control or regulation of property rights, and any attempt to do so would be denounced as going beyond the legitimate activities of the state. C.B. Macpherson (1962: 3) expressed this in terms of possessive individualism, which permeates capitalist society, driven by a 'conception of the individual as essentially the proprietor of his own person or capacities, owing nothing to society for them'.

As for what should replace capitalism, Marxists argue in various ways for the annulment of private property. This is stated clearly, if sporadically, in some of Marx's writings of the early to mid-1840s, where he suggested that in communist society, the achievement of which would require fundamental social change rather than simply political democratization, humans would emancipate themselves from alienation and exploitation. Subsequently, private property would eventually no longer even be desired (Burnham and Lamb, 2019: 59–62, 118, 142–4, 159, 166, 177–9).

Among other socialist ideas on dealing with or replacing property in the new society, those on the moderate, social democratic wing of the ideology hold that pressure from the left can bring about a social and political environment in which such defence is tempered by social justice and an egalitarian sense of community. Social democratic ideas such as those of C.A.R. Crosland and R.H. Tawney can be seen in terms of qualification and regulation of property ownership. Even very moderate social democrats such as Tony Blair have sought some significant restraints on property ownership.

Radical liberals, too, sometimes argue for significant restraints; but to illustrate how socialists differ from such radicals, an influential US liberal thinker should be considered. This is John Rawls, who, in *A Theory of Justice* in 1971, offered a thought experiment. In what he called the original position behind a veil of ignorance, rational individuals would choose two principles of justice. First: 'Each person is to have an equal right to the most extensive total system of equal basic liberties compatible with a similar system of liberty for all.' In a clear indication that individualism underpinned his thought, he stressed that this principle had priority over the second, which consisted of two parts. First, the difference principle holds that social and economic inequalities should be 'to the greatest benefit of the least advantaged, consistent with the just savings principle'. Second, such inequalities should be 'attached to offices and positions open to all under conditions of fair equality of opportunity' (Rawls, 1999: 266). For him, the fair equality of opportunity should have priority over the difference principle. Furthermore, just savings meant that each generation contributes to those in the future and receives from its predecessors (Rawls, 1999: 254). Rawls advocated a democratic state in which government intervention restricts monopolies and regulates firms. The necessary income tax to fund fair equality of opportunity, welfare, education and a social minimum would require property rights to be redefined or readjusted (Rawls, 1999: 243–5).

Rawls (1999: xv–xvi) suggested in the revised edition of his work that his theory could be applicable to a liberal socialist position. Socialists, however, differ from Rawls in that, for them, the right result would require a sense of community. This is because a result based on individual self-interest does not discourage individuals from only just fulfilling the requirements of justice and fairness, rather than seeking to live and work as members of the community.

Chantal Mouffe's notion of 'liberal socialism' contrasts with that of Rawls. Mouffe argues from a socialist position, overlapping liberalism, whilst Rawls starts from a liberal position, overlapping socialism. Mouffe (1993: 100) argues that the associational variant of socialism can preserve the pluralist element of liberal democracy, but that 'this requires a rejection of the atomistic liberal vision of an individual that could exist with her rights and interests prior to and independently of her inscription in a community'. She stresses that this questioning of traditional liberal conceptions of individualism does not mean that, in reviving the social nature of the individual, socialism must revert to the notion of individuals as simply parts of an organic whole. Associational socialism must, she insists, overcome the obstacles that large corporations and centralized big governments put in the path of democracy. For this purpose, a state having primacy over other associations was required in order to bring about democratization. The issue is, she argues, 'how can antagonistic interests be controlled so that no concentration of interests is allowed to exercise a monopoly on economic or political power and dominate the process of decision-making?' (Mouffe, 1993: 99).

Social democrats do consider the issue identified by Mouffe. From the 1950s to the late 1970s, European social democracy tempered the political influence of property owners – even when non-socialist governments were in office (Berki, 1975: 96–7). More radical socialists suggest that social democrats mislead themselves and their supporters, their gains being superficial and temporary, as was witnessed when free-market capitalism was revived in Europe in the late 1970s.

Nevertheless, a pamphlet George Bernard Shaw published anonymously in 1890 for the Fabian Society illustrates the affinities of his relatively moderate position with that of the revolutionaries: 'Socialism is a plan for securing equal rights and opportunities for all. The Socialists are trying to have the land and machinery gradually "socialised", or made the property of the whole people, in order to do away with idle owners, and to win the whole product for those whose labour produces it' (Fabian Society, 1890: 3). Shaw's emphasis on equal opportunities bears a resemblance to Cohen's later argument, discussed in the previous chapter, for socialist equal opportunity, which is far more radical than the liberal version. Shaw's quote illustrates the implications of Cohen's idea in terms of property ownership, as does a passage in *The Communist Manifesto* where Marx and Engels (2002: 235) sum up their theory 'in the single sentence: Abolition of private property'. Having, according to Marx and Engels, derived from workers' labour power, capital was a collective product owned by the exploiting class. 'When, therefore', they suggested, 'capital is converted into common property, into the property of all members of society, personal property is not thereby transformed into social property. It is only the social character of the property that is changed. It loses its class character' (Marx and Engels, 2002: 236). While Shaw's socialism clearly differed from that of Marx and Engels, there are some remarkable similarities in terms of property ownership. Shaw, Marx and Engels have influenced many subsequent socialists. Discussing these three thinkers' views on property has helped pave the way for an examination of twentieth- and twenty-first-century socialist views regarding how the economy should be constituted in the new society.

The socialist state and the economy

Chapter 5 of this book will examine some influential socialist blueprints for a new society. Each focuses in part on the economy. The present section looks more broadly at three categories of socialist economy: Marxist-Leninist, social democratic and associationalist.

The command economy of actually existing socialism

After the Bolshevik revolution, the USSR stood almost alone as a communist/socialist state in a world dominated by capitalism. This began to change after the Second World War when, under pressure from Moscow, a number of Eastern European countries adopted Marxism-Leninism. The states and economies of these countries varied but, except for Yugoslavia, which broke away from the bloc, they adopted central command economies of what came to be known as actually existing socialism.

In his 1952 pamphlet *Economic Problems of Socialism in the USSR*, Stalin sought to provide a theoretical underpinning of the central command economy in terms of the objective character of laws. One category of supposedly objective laws was that of political economy, the processes of which, according to Stalin's misconstrual of Marx, 'operate independently of the will of man' (Stalin, 1972: 2). For Stalin, just as laws of nature could be restricted and redirected in the service of society, such as the building of dams and hydro-electric power stations, so could the laws of political economy in periods of capitalism and socialism be utilized, restricted and harnessed in different ways – although perhaps it would have been more honest for him to say that the theory of such laws could be 'reinterpreted and manipulated' rather than suggesting the laws themselves could be redirected.

Unlike laws of science, Stalin (1972: 4) insisted, those of political economy are impermanent. Laws of political economy would not be abolished but, rather, 'lose their validity owing to the new economic conditions', their place being taken by new laws arising from those conditions. Stalin ignored the human-made nature of economic laws, which thus cannot be objective. If they were objective, moreover, they could not be replaced with new economic laws. The absurdity of Stalin's theory was noted the following year from within the Marxist tradition by Isaac Deutscher (1953: 360), who described the Soviet leader's insistence on the validity of economic laws under socialism as 'turgid scholasticism'. Stalin's theory amounted, in other words, to tedious, narrow-minded insistence on doctrine.

Stalin employed the Marxist argument that the development of productive forces such as human capabilities, tools, technology and science requires economic conditions which overcome the restraints that capitalism imposes. Socialization of the means of production, which takes particular forms applicable to the state of development of the society in question, does utilize those forces. There may, for example, be public ownership at both the national and local level. The extent of the nationalized and collectivist sectors would also vary according to the size, levels of economic development, demographics, and so on, of each country. The form that emerged in the USSR reflected what Stalin portrayed as an alliance of the proletariat and a large peasantry, making it unreasonable to take the agricultural sector into ownership at the national level. Hence, whilst industry would be state-owned, agriculture would continue with commodity production organized into large-scale collective farms, albeit controlled by the state and thereby supplied 'with first-class tractors and other machines' (Stalin, 1972: 13). This would involve central planning, which would master and apply what Stalin (1972: 7) called 'the economic law of balanced development of the national economy'. As Deutscher (1953: 360) suggested, the notion that objective economic laws can be replaced by new ones was also significant in that it indicated Stalin's desire to keep change under control and forestall radical economic policy – hardly a Marxist position.

Stalin's pamphlet portrayed economic laws as having some sort of independent existence, when in fact they were the result of collective human actions over time. He acknowledged that developments in productive forces can make what is perceived as a law outdated. What, however, he ignored (intentionally or otherwise) was that other human-based forces can also have this effect.

Perhaps most significantly, Stalin and the socialist economic system that survived his death in 1953 ignored the value that suitably regulated market forces can have in terms of efficiency, productivity, incentives and innovation. Market forces are, of course, a human creation; an acknowledgement that the humans involved in their operations deserve suitable rewards would reduce or even eliminate the alienation and exploitation that a loosely regulated free-market system produces.

Alec Nove (1991: 73–126) presented a major critique of the USSR and the Eastern European countries for ignoring the advantages of a regulated market. From his non-Marxist left position, he criticized Marxism-Leninism during its period of decline in the 1980s. As will be seen later in the present chapter, he advocated an economic system that fits loosely into a tradition that has come to be known as market socialism.

Some of the Marxist-Leninist states in Eastern Europe attempted to vary the centralist model to take account of particular circumstances. Collectivist agricultural policies were sometimes implemented alongside ownership and control of industry at the national level. This was even the case in the relatively highly industrialized German Democratic Republic (GDR), where private farming, while never abolished, was expected to wither away due to the success of collectivized agriculture in the county. This demise never happened and from the 1970s onwards the GDR accepted private farming as a contributor to production in the country, but without bringing it within a cohesive plan (Brezinski, 1990). The Marxist-Leninist state and its bureaucracy tended to ignore the problems that its economy faced.

Another feature of the Marxist-Leninist countries was the suppression of dissenting voices: a situation that continues in those that remain. This suppression helped enable the Stalinist model to spread and survive throughout much of Eastern Europe from the late 1940s until the end of the 1980s. The Yugoslav Communists broke with the USSR in 1948 and eventually helped found the international non-aligned movement. Nevertheless, the suppression continued in Yugoslavia, where one of the most influential dissidents was Milovan Djilas. Having been a high-ranking member of Yugoslavia's ruling Communist Party, he drew attention to the problems the Marxist-Leninist states were digging themselves further into before his criticism brought about his demotion and imprisonment; he eventually left the party. In the 1950s, he claimed to be closer to democratic socialism than communism (Djilas, 1957: vi). The Yugoslav leader Josip Broz Tito had broken away from Stalin's hegemony in the late 1940s and thereafter Yugoslavia had developed its own economic model based on decentralization and workers' self-management. Djilas (1957: 68) said this was merely a concession by which the Communist Party leaders and bureaucracy sought legitimacy to bolster their own positions. Similar concessions, he suggested, had been offered elsewhere in Eastern Europe. Djilas argued that a new class had emerged in the communist states, including his own, as the leaders and bureaucrats had begun to operate in their own interests. This class had established its own power over society, even though its members may well have believed that such power would eventually result in happiness and freedom for all (Djilas, 1957: 38). As a socialist, he stressed that he was not criticizing egalitarian ideas, which had 'existed in varying forms since human society began – and which contemporary Communism accepts in word'. After all, these were 'principles to which fighters for progress and freedom will always aspire' (Djilas, 1957: vii). His point was that however much communists in power claimed, and perhaps in some cases even believed, that their rule was fostering a society based on equality and community, in fact they had become a new ruling class enjoying a position of domination.

In Djilas' view, a fundamental problem that would eventually lead to the demise of the communist states was that, as the new class established its position and power, the development of the economy reflected that of the regime 'from a dictatorship of the proletariat to a reactionary despotism'. The interference of government in the economy had originally been necessary for rapid industrialization, but had become 'a vital, personal interest on the part of the ruling bureaucrats'. Economic development had 'come to be guided mainly in the interests of the ruling class' (Djilas, 1957: 103). The time would inevitably come, Djilas (1957: 69) predicted, when 'the new class leaves the historical scene'.

Just over thirty years later, Djilas' prediction was proven to be accurate, at least in the USSR and Eastern Europe. In the 1980s, the new Soviet leader Mikhail Gorbachev warned his comrades of impending problems not unlike those which Djilas had foreseen. Gorbachev introduced his arguments for *perestroika* and *glasnost*. A loss of momentum had, he suggested, become particularly clear in the latter half of the previous decade as economic failures became increasingly frequent. This brought about what he called a 'braking mechanism' which impeded social and economic development at the very time at which new advancements in science and technology were making progress possible (Gorbachev, 1988: 18–19). *Glasnost* broadly translates as openness, and Gorbachev warned that this was necessary if communists were to be honest with both themselves and their citizens and thus prepare for and eventually legitimate extensive reform. *Glasnost* was thus needed to create the environment of *perestroika*, which meant restructuring, especially of the communist economy.

Gorbachev (1988: 32) was enthusiastic about fundamental reform of the Soviet economic system by means of 'broad democratization of all aspects of society'. Involving 'mass initiative', which would overcome stagnation and counter the braking mechanism, *perestroika* was 'the comprehensive development of democracy, socialist self-government, encouragement of initiative and creative endeavour, improved order and discipline, more glasnost, criticism and self-criticism in all spheres of our society' (Gorbachev, 1988: 34). Gorbachev (1988: 33–4) envisaged 'radical reorganization of centralized economic management'. Unfortunately, he provided hardly any detail and there was little clear planning in evidence. *Glasnost* and *perestroika* were insufficient to save Marxism-Leninism in the USSR and Eastern Europe. The collapse of the Eastern European regimes in the revolutions of 1989–90 was soon followed by the disintegration of Yugoslavian communism in the Balkan wars of the 1990s. The Communist Party of the Soviet Union itself fell from power in the early years of that decade, was temporarily banned and re-emerged as a shadow of its former self in opposition. The Marxist-Leninist parties of Eastern Europe were transformed into social democratic ones, with varying degrees of success.

The state and the economy in social democracy

A key figure in the evolution of social democracy into the second main pillar of socialism in the twentieth century was Eduard Bernstein, who sought in 1899 to bring Marx's work up to date. Bernstein challenged what he called the 'catastrophe theory' that Marx and Engels had expressed in *The Communist Manifesto* and which their followers had taken for granted. Capitalism would not collapse in the short term but instead assume new and unforeseen forms. Evidence was, Bernstein argued, already beginning to appear. In societies where capitalism was relatively highly developed, the number of property owners and capitalists had increased rather than diminished. Democratic institutions had begun to emerge through which a social reaction could be expressed which would deny the bourgeoisie the political privilege they had previously enjoyed and allow the labour movement to challenge capitalist exploitation (Bernstein, 1993: 1–3).

Bernstein (1993: 28) acknowledged the influence of Lassalle, who, as was discussed earlier in the present chapter, had anticipated the capacity of the state to bring about such reform of the capitalist economy. Essentially, Bernstein was arguing that for the foreseeable future, social democrats should work within capitalism, using the state to secure regulation which would put limits on the power of property ownership. By means of such limitation, the inequalities allowed by the capitalist economy could be reduced significantly.

A social democratic position bearing distinct affinities with that of Bernstein was voiced by G.D.H. Cole at the end of the 1920s in *The Next Ten Years in British Social and Economic Policy*. Previously a prominent associational socialist, he declared that the 'need for fresh thinking is urgent' (Cole, 1929: 419). Accepting that social change would be gradual in the short term, at a time when intellectuals were turning away from socialism and embracing individualism, he called for moderation. This did not, he stressed, mean his fundamental views had changed. What had changed were the problems to which those views were applied. Although the Labour Party had become a major force with the distinct capability of taking power by parliamentary means (as would indeed happen later that year), the settlement of the First World War and the depression meant that socialism had become a matter of practical politics rather than perfection (Cole, 1929: vii–viii).

Practicality had important implications for socialization, which Cole (1929: 133) defined as 'the extension of some kind of effective social control' over both 'the economic system as a whole' and 'all such parts of it as vitally affect the conduct of the whole'. This need involve neither nationalization nor the direct administration of industries and services. Socialism, he stressed, attacks 'the dominance of capitalism in the life of society' rather than 'each and every instance of private property' (Cole, 1929: 132).

A decade after Cole published *The Next Ten Years*, the Swedish social democrat Ernst Wigforss produced a detailed article on the problems of conventional capitalist economics and the merits of his country's then-developing social democratic alternative. His article of 1938 serves as a good indication of the key ideas behind the Swedish social democratic model, which achieved considerable electoral success for much of the remainder of the twentieth century.

Wigforss argued that the attempt to achieve a balance each year between total income and expenses, which had for a long time been considered the only sound fiscal policy, was 'full of contradictions', exceptions sometimes being made for purposes such as defence and measures to repair a failing economy. This policy, which considered public expenditure a burden on economic life and society, was, he observed, 'abandoned during the recent depression period, simultaneously with the rise of new conceptions of the influence which the state can exert upon economic change by means of its financial policy' (Wigforss, 1938: 27). In 1933 and 1936, his Swedish Social Democratic Workers' Party formed minority governments which, with the support of two communist parties, increased taxation and public borrowing to fund welfare, education, economic expansion, public capital investment in infrastructure, utilities, housing and income-yielding state enterprises such as agriculture. By 1938, this programme was achieving a balanced budget in a way conservatives and liberals had not thought possible. As Wigforss (1938: 33) put it: 'Apprehensions that a policy of borrowing funds for unproductive expenses would increase the burden of the public debt and undermine confidence in the state's finances have thus proved groundless.' Marxists argue that social democracy must always work within limits allowed by capitalism, and that the state ultimately protects capitalism from fundamental change. Wigforss' discussion of the achievements of his own party serves to illustrate that much can be achieved within those limits.

Nevertheless, a problem with social democracy is, according to the contemporary socialist thinker Hilary Wainwright, that it is paternalistic, having 'been built around – at best – a benevolent version of the understanding of power-as-domination'. This, she adds, 'has often involved a low estimation of people's capabilities by the experts responsible for policy making' (Wainwright, 2018: 13). This is a problem that the associationalist tradition within socialism has sought to avoid.

Associational socialism

Many socialists have found associationalism – or pluralism as it is sometimes called, because of the plurality of effective associations – an attractive alternative to Marxism-Leninism and social democracy. In the early twentieth century, for example, Harold Laski, the English guild socialists and French syndicalists offered several suggestions as to how this might be achieved (Laborde, 2000: 140–53). The roots of the associationalist tradition can, however, be traced back to the ideas of Fourier in the early nineteenth century.

Fourier (1996: 36–7) argued that all other physical movements in the world could be accounted for by one or more of the following four: social movement (concerning social mechanisms), animal movement (concerning the passions and instincts of all animals, including the human), organic movement (concerning properties such as form, colour and smell) and material movement (concerning gravitation of matter). Significantly, these four movements could explain the natural drive he called 'passionate attraction'. On this basis, social relations could be regulated, and agricultural association introduced as the type of industry necessary for satisfactory human life (Fourier, 1996: 15–18).

Fourier (1996: 10) believed his theory could solve the problems of existing civilization, which was 'bathing in blood in order to appease mercantile jealousies'. The problems included poverty, and he placed particular emphasis on women in this respect (Fourier, 1996: 91–3, 129–43). His proposed solution was based on associative agricultural communities he called phalanxes. Each phalanx of around a thousand people would cultivate a canton comprising a number of progressive series, each consisting of 'several associated groups entirely devoted to the different branches of a single industry' (Fourier, 1996: 12). 'Once established in a single canton', agricultural association would 'be imitated spontaneously in every country, simply by virtue of the vast profits and numberless pleasures this order will guarantee all individuals, however rich or poor they may be' (Fourier, 1996: 15). This would 'cause wars, revolutions, poverty and injustice to disappear' (Fourier, 1996: 88). Mercantile jealousies would be overcome permanently without the need for combat, and 'maritime might, hitherto so powerful', would 'sink into absolute oblivion' (Fourier, 1996: 10).

While clearly advocating community as a means to emancipation, Fourier (1996: 13) had no time for theoretical or philosophical arguments for equality. He was critical of the French revolutionaries' egalitarian ideals of liberal, formal equality of rights before the law (Arblaster, 1984: 203–11). The revolution driven by this cause of equality was, for Fourier (1996: 280), a fantasy, which did little to improve the lives of ordinary people, many of whom died both within France and in wars abroad. His new society would require pure, ardent passions rather than philosophical arguments for equality (Fourier, 1996: 13).

Each series in the cantons would, in Fourier's scheme, 'be composed of people who are unequal in every way: in age, fortune, character, understanding, etc.' Inequality of condition would be beneficial because of competition between the series – between pear growers and apple growers, for example – to produce more and better goods in a condition of social harmony. Work would become pleasure, people being more concerned with competing than making profit (Fourier, 1996: 292–3). More and better goods would be produced for all.

In the 1818 edition of *The Four Movements*, Fourier (1996: 312) conceded that he had 'forgotten the Aromal Movement' and 'mistakenly situated the passional on the line of the four others, when it is their Pivot and their model'. What he meant was later clarified by his follower Albert Brisbane (1840: iii) in a book written to present Fourier's ideas to the American public. Brisbane (1840: 161–2) listed Fourier's five movements as the 'material', 'aromal', 'organic', 'industrial' and 'social and passionate'. The industrial was the animal in Fourier's original classification. The aromal comprised forces such as electricity, heat, light, galvanism and magnetism, and perhaps this indicates that Fourier came in 1818 to see the benefits of galvanism in producing electricity, heat and light to the communities he proposed. Fourier can thus be read as meaning by 'passional' the passions of humans in their relations. In his communities, association and cooperation would bring about greater rewards than achievable in the existing, exploitative civilization and produce a far more egalitarian society.

Like Fourier and Brisbane, later in the nineteenth century and early in the twentieth the French syndicalists rejected their country's revolutionary tradition with its focus on citizenship. Like the North American industrial unionists, the most well-known organization of which was the Industrial Workers of the World (IWW), the syndicalists in France and other European countries rejected orthodox politics such as parliamentary participation and focused on producers rather than citizens. Each, furthermore, sought to abolish the existing capitalist order and the state. Advocating direct action by trade unionists, if necessary against the formal leadership of their unions, the syndicalists and industrial unionists aimed for a general strike (Darlington, 2013).

Syndicalist plans for the future society were more complex than those of the industrial unionists. While the industrial unionists of the IWW advocated central control, the European syndicalists advocated federations of groups of associated workers (Jennings, 1991; Peterson, 1981). Some members of the IWW took their message to the UK and influenced some of the radical socialists there in a climate of industrial unrest in the first two decades of the twentieth century (Pelling, 1956: 99–105).

Acknowledging that it had been inspired in part by American industrial unionism and French syndicalism, Cole suggested in *Self-Government in Industry* that the national guilds movement sought to bring about this revolution in a less radical manner more suited to British conditions and temperaments (Cole, 1917: 6). Signs were emerging that after the world war the great capitalists would seek to break the power of the trade unions. Revolutionary change in the control of industry and in society more generally was thus needed, political democracy being 'a farce and a pretence, because industrial aristocracy remains almost unchallenged' (Cole, 1917: 3). Believing the British working class would not accept socialism dominated by the national level of government, Cole's guild socialist alternative would require the working class to build a new economic system to replace capitalism by means of a new network of organizations in which control of industry would be shared between producers and consumers in the community. Such control would be democratized, meaning 'the workers themselves should have an ever-increasing measure of power and responsibility in control, and that capitalist supremacy can be overthrown only by a system of industrial democracy in which the workers will control industry in conjunction with a democratised state' (Cole, 1917: 4). As will be discussed in

Chapter 5, in 1920 he developed these ideas as a blueprint for a socialist society in *Guild Socialism Restated*.

Laski's associationalism was inextricably related to his critique of sovereignty. The link is clear in the first two of the essays he published in *The Foundations of Sovereignty and Other Essays*. In the title essay, he argued that the concept of the sovereign state, portrayed as it was as the ultimate source of authority operating without a superior at the national level of government for the protection of the demands of the universal interests of the community, in fact served to conceal the relations of power (Laski, 1921: 1–29). In the essay 'On the Problem of Administrative Areas', he argued that the holders of economic power wielded power at every geographical level in both the centralized parliamentary system of the UK and the federal system of the USA. For him, geographical levels of government should have a stronger role in providing for the shared needs of people in their respective areas. This would be accompanied by a system of functional units responsible for the special interests of groups, including the trade unions. With a more extensive education, union members would be able to negotiate with their employers, leading eventually to the replacement of capitalism by a new economic system featuring industrial democracy. Once the real purpose of sovereignty had been exposed, the central government could and should play a genuine role in ensuring that the functional bodies did not defend their own interests at the expense of others (Laski, 1921: 30–102).

Laski gradually moderated but, like Cole, never entirely abandoned associationalism. In *A Grammar of Politics*, he proposed the retention of a significant amount of control by people in their working lives, but now saw a more extensive economic role for the state (Laski, 1925: 433–540). In the 1930s, however, as he witnessed the spread of fascism and other events and processes detrimental to the advance of socialism, he adopted a quasi-Marxist view. In an introductory essay to the fourth edition of *A Grammar of Politics* he continued to call for a combination of parliamentary organization and functional distribution of some authority but warned that, because of capitalist domination of the sovereign state, success was far less likely than he had previously thought (Laski, 1938: x–xxvii).

In the 1970s, Poulantzas presented an argument which bore affinities with Laski's modified associationalism of the mid-1920s. In *State, Power, Socialism*, he moved away from the structural Marxism of his early works. Conceding that liberal democratic critiques of Marxism needed to be taken seriously, he criticized both social democracy and Marxism-Leninism for being 'marked by statism and profound distrust of mass initiatives, in short by suspicion of democratic demands' (Poulantzas, 1978: 251). Lenin's abolition of representative democracy had brought about not a direct democracy by means of self-management in the soviets in which workers would make their own decisions but, rather, authoritarian direction from the centre: 'And so was Stalinist statism born' (Poulantzas, 1978: 255). Given that a state is needed to oversee the direct democracy of self-management, Stalinist domination remained a likely result should representative democracy be abolished in other countries. The social democratic alternative, however, involved a new 'enlightened' 'left elite' operating through representative democracy in a system which 'left as understood that the State will thereby bring socialism to the popular masses from above' (Poulantzas, 1978: 255). Hence, Poulantzas presented an associationalist argument instead. For him, the transformation of the state would need to involve the introduction of genuine direct democracy through self-management institutions and also the extension of the political freedoms that representative democracy allowed. He did not, however, offer a plan for the institutional arrangements he considered necessary for the new socialist economy to operate.

As will be discussed in Chapter 5, in post-Second World War Yugoslavia, writers such as Edvard Kardelj offered theories of socialist self-management. They combined associationalism with a vanguard Leninist and Stalinist line that had usually been applied and put into practice in the form of the authoritarian command economy. Poulantzas did not mention Yugoslavia but, while he did not entirely abandon Marxism, as had Djilas, it seems likely that for not entirely different reasons he, too, would have been dissatisfied with this implementation of socialist self-management.

In the 1980s and 1990s, Paul Hirst helped revive associationalist socialism. An associationalist economy, he suggested in his paper 'Associational Socialism in a Pluralist State', could appeal in Western society, where because of change over time the traditional classes were no longer as clearly defined, and the popularity of socialist central planning had waned. If put into practice in Western societies, associational socialism would, he argued, be compatible with Western civil society, enhance the power of voluntary associations and communities, and thus build on rather than negate plurality and diversity. 'Unlike the economic totalitarianism of central planning', he stressed, associational socialism was 'not condemned to marginalise associations and deny them decision-making autonomy'. Nevertheless, associational socialism did not involve the domination inherent in market-oriented corporate capitalism because it 'does not push associations to the "social" margins, away from economic market-oriented activity' (Hirst, 1988: 142). Like Laski, he believed that, to be socialist, an associational society would need 'regulation and supra-enterprise services and agencies in order to function' (Hirst, 1988: 143). A competitive market would otherwise eventually be transformed into corporate capitalism.

By the late twentieth century, with hindsight of the decline and eventual collapse of the centrally planned economy in communist, Marxist-Leninist states, the view that it was futile to seek a non-market economy in modern industrial society became hugely influential. The failure of central planning was deemed almost inevitable when economies grew more complex. This was because of, first, the need for more information than a centrally planned system can provide in a complex economy; second, the need for incentives to make innovative decisions, take risks, make harsh but necessary decisions and work harder than necessary; and, third, the problem of authoritarian tendencies that central planning fostered. The free-market economist F.A. Hayek argued that these were problems that made any kind of socialism unviable and ethically reprehensible (Caldwell, 1997).

In the 1980s and early 1990s, Nove (1991: 207) disagreed with Hayek, proposing a feasible socialism which has a distinct associational element. For Nove, the large-scale means of production should largely be owned by the state at the national level or by cooperatives, private ownership being very limited. There would be central planning guided by a democratically elected assembly, supplemented by referenda to make some decisions on what goods should be produced and services provided. Decisions would thus be influenced by the market. Workers and consumers would also be involved with management in decision-making at various levels within each sector, except for in the limited, small-scale private sector. Decisions on taxation, income policies and restraining monopoly power would continue to be made by government at the national level (Nove, 1991: 24–6).

Nove's model would soon be overshadowed by the 'Third Way'. As discussed in the Introduction, moderate social democrats adopted 'Third Way' thinking with, at least temporarily, considerable enthusiasm from voters in countries including the UK and Germany. Nevertheless, Nove's case against central planning and for market principles continued to have influence.

Nove's 'feasible' socialism bore affinities with a tradition of thought known as market socialism, several models of which exist. Oskar Lange (1964) was an early market socialist theorist, arguing in *On the Economic Theory of Socialism* of 1938 for a central planning board and a distribution of the management of socialized enterprises with free choice of occupation. Management would respond to consumer demand, but in a situation of scarcity the board would manipulate prices so as to distribute in ways which delivered the maximum social welfare.

Later market socialists, such as John Roemer, David Schweickart and David Miller offered less centralized versions than that of Lange. For Roemer (1992: 452–5), large firms would be publicly owned and run by managers either elected by workers or appointed by boards of directors. The goal of the managers would be to maximize profits. Prices of products would be determined by the market. Profits and wages would be taxed to enable the government to provide public goods such as water and services such as health. This would be a socialist system for two main reasons. First, the party elected to government would have the power to intervene in the economy in terms of deciding on how funds should be invested. Second, profits generated from the operation of the system would contribute, after taxation, to a central fund divided on approximately equal terms as dividends among citizens.

Schweickart's version does not involve egalitarian ownership of the means of production at the national level. Instead workers in an enterprise are associates who self-manage it through elected representatives. Their enterprise pays rent (a form of tax) for access to social property. He suggests this use of taxation to fund investment is more reliable than having continually to persuade citizens to save money. The investment goes to communities in the country according to their size, shared among enterprises partly on the basis of profitability and partly on how many people are employed. Schweickart calls his model 'economic democracy', which 'may be thought of as an economic system with three basic structures, worker self-management of enterprises, social control of investment, and a market for goods and services'. This differs from capitalism, which is based on 'wage labour, private ownership of the means of production, and a market for goods services, capital, and labor' (Schweickart, 1998: 18).

Miller wants to avoid a heavy tax burden, which does not guarantee significantly greater equality, and for this reason relies on savings by citizens for investment. The key idea of his version is 'that the market mechanism is retained as a means of providing most goods and services, while the ownership of capital is socialized' (Miller, 1990: 10). All the productive enterprises would be workers' cooperatives, leasing capital from an investment agency such as a bank. The cooperatives would be democratically controlled by their workers. Decisions would include how to distribute profits in the cooperative, including salaries. The cooperatives would make their own decisions on issues such as what products to make, methods and prices.

But how well does market socialism actually meet the key principles of socialism? Does it produce a less unequal outcome than a capitalist market economy? Does it foster community? Does market freedom enable social freedom to flourish? Market socialism would need to be compared with other forms of socialism on these criteria.

Associationalist ideas remained of interest to socialists in the early twenty-first century. Wainwright, for example, published a study of a public service project in the British city Newcastle-on-Tyne, where civil service workers organized themselves, with the support of their trade union, to provide a more successful service than had outsourcing arrangements in which public services were hived off to the private sector. This, she argued, involved 'real participation and empowerment' (Wainwright with Little, 2009: 169).

Socialist self-management in Yugoslavia and guild socialism in the UK are among the examples to be discussed in Chapter 5, which focuses on notable blueprints for a new socialist society. First, however, socialist ideas on political and social change will be considered.

4
Political and Social Change

Socialists differ significantly, and often quarrel, about the nature and detail of transition to a better society and polity. One division concerns the extent of political, social and economic change with which socialists are or would be satisfied. Another division concerns whether the means should be direct and revolutionary or constitutional. While these two divisions often correlate with one another, this is not necessarily the case, as will be discussed in the next section. In the section after that, another sort of difference is considered: the extent to which people need to be guided or led into their new society.

There are also differences among strategies for bringing about political and social change within the broader divisions. While Marx, Lenin, Rosa Luxemburg, Leon Trotsky and Mao are important representatives of the revolutionary tradition, their ideas were quite distinct from one another. Sidney and Beatrice Webb, Eduard Bernstein and R.H. Tawney are among the many on the reformist wing, which, too, is rich in its diversity. As we have already seen, there are aspects of reform and revolution in some theories, such as those of Harold Laski, Antonio Gramsci, Nicos Poulantzas and some of the later works of Marx. This chapter focuses on some of these differences within the broad category of socialism.

Revolutionary or constitutional change

A particular means of change employed by a party or group need not be specific to a single ideology. The reason for taking action in the first place is crucial to its ideological location. Indeed, revolutions such as the French in 1789, the Iranian 190 years later and those in Eastern Europe a decade after that were not socialist ones. To be socialist, the campaign must be entered into by people who believe they and their communities can and should be allowed to flourish in cooperation with one another; that this requires particular sorts of equality and freedom; that people have responsibility to ensure that the possible sociality is maintained; and that capitalism needs to be either substantially reformed or abolished.

Another pertinent question is whether the process of change should lead to the eventual abolition of the state altogether. Engels (1976: 363) said that the state will wither away, or in other words die out, rather than be abolished. This serves as an example of ideological overlap, this time with anarchism. While agreeing with anarchists that the state will at some point cease to exist, Marxist socialists such as Engels accept that some form of state is necessary for the foreseeable future. Anarchists tend to call for a swifter abolition or destruction of the state rather than a withering way. The distinction between anarchists and revolutionary Marxist socialists can be appreciated by means of a view expressed by Lenin. He drew the socialist/anarchist distinction in *The State and Revolution* shortly before he and his Russian communists seized power in October 1917. First, according to Lenin (1976: 137), whilst, like anarchists, they aimed for the complete destruction of the state, Marxists recognized 'that this aim can only be achieved after classes have been abolished by the socialist revolution, as the result of the establishment of socialism, which leads to the withering away of the state'. Anarchists, he argued, failed to understand the conditions in which the destruction of the state could take place, wanting 'to destroy the state completely overnight'. Second, Lenin went on, while Marxists and anarchists agreed that the old state must be destroyed, the former recognized that after conquering the state power and demolishing its machine they must substitute for it a new state machine 'consisting of an organization of the armed workers'. Whilst anarchists rejected the state, they, according to Lenin, had 'absolutely no idea' what the proletariat should put in its place. Third, according to Lenin, Marxists 'demand that use be made of the present-day state in preparing the proletariat for revolution: the anarchists reject this'. Although anarchists would challenge his criticism of them, Lenin's distinction does help one to identify a clear difference between socialism and anarchism. It serves, moreover, to indicate that it would be better to locate those who are sometimes deemed anarchist socialists firmly in the anarchist category while noting the overlap.

The very general division between those socialists who (a) seek to overthrow and replace the entire capitalist system and its political institutions and those who (b) seek to reform that system by constitutional means is far from all-encompassing. Thinkers such as Robert Owen and Charles Fourier who assumed that socialist communities and federations could be built within existing states are neglected by this division. Whilst, moreover, it is often the case that revolutionaries who seek to overthrow the existing order by unconstitutional and sometimes violent means usually want more extensive change than even the most radical of social democrats countenance, this correlation does not always apply. Sometimes the democratic socialists want eventually to bring about change just as far reaching as do the direct revolutionaries, or even indeed more so. Ferdinand Lassalle (1990), for example, insisted that the only way for the working class to see its broader demands realized, rather than simply achieve improvements, would be by means of representation in the national legislature. For this purpose, the working class would need to form its own political party and campaign through lawful agitation for universal suffrage, leading to the empowerment of that party. Without such a party, Lassalle argued, the working class could achieve no more than amelioration of its conditions.

Constitutional paths to a better society would take time to produce results. As Bernstein (1993: 207) conceded in 1899, 'you can not in the course of a couple of years move the entire working class into conditions which are substantially different from those in which it finds itself at present'. The revolutionary approach was stronger on the negative side, he acknowledged, working 'more quickly where it is a question of removing obstacles which a privileged minority places in the path of progress'. Constitutional legislation, however, while slower, was more powerful 'where it is a question of creating permanent and viable economic arrangements' (Bernstein, 1993: 204). He summarized his case for taking the constitutional path as follows: 'As soon as a nation has reached a political state of affairs where the rights of the propertied minority have ceased to be a serious impediment to social progress, where the negative tasks of political action take second place to the positive, the appeal to violent revolution becomes pointless' (Bernstein, 1993: 205). Bernstein and Lassalle each thus believed that gradual political change could produce significant, fundamental and indeed far-reaching social results.

Thinkers such as Trotsky have criticized as unrealistic the social democratic belief that constitutional change could bring about substantial results, and in 1917, Trotsky persuaded Lenin that, rather than lead Russia into a post-revolutionary period of capitalist development, a socialist revolution should begin immediately. This was part of his theory of permanent revolution (Service, 2010: 108–9, 161–9). Trotsky insisted that revolutionaries needed to seize the moment when a sufficiently sizeable part of the populace was prepared for swift, direct action. As he put it in 1930, in the preface to *The History of the Russian Revolution*: 'For decades the oppositional criticism is nothing more than a safety valve for mass dissatisfaction, a condition of the stability of the social structure' (Trotsky, 1977: 18). Social democratic criticism, he went on, served such a purpose. Five years earlier, in *Where is Britain Going?*, he argued that the Labour Party, by limiting itself to Fabian gradualism and parliamentary politics, was strengthening the confidence of the bourgeoisie and stretching to the limit the endurance of the British proletariat. 'The longer the Fabians restrain the revolutionary development of Britain', he stressed, 'the more threatening and raging will be the explosion' (Trotsky, 1970: 133).

Lenin, too, rejected the reformism which 'social democracy'

has since come to signify, even though at the beginning of the twentieth century he, like other Marxists, referred to himself as a social democrat. In *What is to be Done?* of 1902 he summed up the mood which was leading to a redefinition of social democracy:

> Social-Democracy must change from a party of social revolution into a democratic party of social reforms. Bernstein has surrounded this political demand with a whole battery of well-attuned 'new' arguments and reasonings. … Thus, the demand for a decisive turn from revolutionary Social-Democracy to bourgeois social-reformism was accompanied by a no less decisive turn towards bourgeois criticism of all the fundamental ideas of Marxism. (Lenin, 1947: 9)

Fifteen years later, focusing on the programmatic demand of the German Social Democrats of the 1870s for a 'free people's state', Lenin argued in *The State and Revolution* that this amounted to 'an opportunistic slogan; for it expressed not only an embellishment of bourgeois democracy, but also a failure to understand the socialist criticism of the state in general'. A bourgeois democratic state was, he went on, 'the best form of the state for the proletariat under capitalism; but we have no right to forget that wage slavery is the lot of the people even in the most democratic bourgeois republic' (Lenin, 1976: 24). 'The supersession of the bourgeois state by the proletarian state is impossible', he insisted, 'without a violent revolution' (Lenin 1976: 27).

In the mid-twentieth century, C.A.R. Crosland disagreed fundamentally with Marxists such as Lenin. Revolution, for Crosland, was no longer a relevant strategy, especially in countries such as the UK where significant progress was being made by parliamentary means regarding equality of opportunity and social mobility. Nevertheless, Crosland was not content with those achievements. As he put it:

> They need … to be combined with measures … to equalise the distribution of rewards and privileges so as to diminish the degree of class stratification, the injustice of large inequalities, and the collective discontents which come from too great a dispersion of rewards. The limited goal is not, from a socialist point of view, sufficient. (Crosland, 1956: 237)

While Crosland thus called for the diminishment of class stratification rather than the abolition of class, his suggestions imply that in other respects he was as ambitious as Lenin regarding change. Crosland's views on the extent of achievable change will feature in the next chapter of this book, in what can be seen as his blueprint for a new society.

Another indication that social democrats sometimes seek extensive change can be found in G.D.H. Cole's later work, in which he had moderated his earlier guild socialist radicalism. In *The Next Ten Years* he offered the following summary of how a socialist would view the question of how to deal with capitalism: 'He wants Socialism to occupy the key positions in the economic order which are now in capitalist hands. Within the system of Socialist control, he recognises fully the need for a great diversity in the actual forms of enterprise, and for a wide freedom to experiment in new ways of organisation' (Cole, 1929: 132). Now this would be rather too radical for some social democrats, and indeed far too radical for moderates such as Tony Blair. Nevertheless, Cole's approach in 1929 helps show that some social democrats are far more radical than others in terms of the extent of plans for change.

Disagreements within socialism between revolutionaries and social democrats do not therefore necessarily mean that revolutionaries seek a greater extent of desired change. As we saw in the case of Bernstein, in some cases, the aim may be to eventually abolish capitalism by a long-term series of reforms. One cannot, therefore, simply equate revolutionary socialism with a demand for extensive change and social democracy with less extensive reform.

The traditional revolutionary–parliamentary division is of limited value for other reasons too. First, it does not take into consideration the extent to which socialists expect people to be either led, on the one hand, or encouraged to act for themselves, on the other. Some revolutionaries expect people to use their own initiative while others stress the need for leadership; some socialists who advocate constitutional activity in parliamentary terms insist on firm direction by a party while others encourage grassroots activism. Second, the traditional division does not take into account approaches which consider that neither revolutionary nor constitutional change will get to the heart of the problems unless the hegemonic power that underpins dominance and exploitation in the existing order is countered. Let us examine these two divisions.

The role of the people

Some influential socialists of various persuasions have argued that ordinary people need to be guided by strong leadership. Within the revolutionary Marxist tradition, Lenin (1947: 78–93) pioneered the idea, which became prominent in Marxism-Leninism, that revolution required a small, disciplined and dedicated party operating as the vanguard. Among social democrats, early Fabians such as George Bernard Shaw and Sidney Webb presented their competing doctrines of permeation, Shaw looking to persuade radical members of the Liberal Party to transfer to a new socialist party he hoped would be formed, Webb seeking instead to persuade the Liberal Party itself to adopt socialist policies. In each version, socialist intellectuals would gradually infiltrate, or permeate, the decision-making process of states by influencing reformist liberal politicians and radical social activists, among others (Bevir, 2011: 196–201). Lenin, Webb and Shaw thus each believed that strong guidance was needed from socialist intellectuals.

Some socialists take the very different view that to achieve significant change, people must be sufficiently dissatisfied with the existing order to attempt some kind of action themselves. It is not just revolutionary theorists who stress this necessity for people to act upon the feeling of discontent without waiting for orders from the vanguard. Some who are committed to using the electoral system of their country stress the need for ordinary people to spark the movement and generate similar feelings among a sizeable part of the electorate. In the early twenty-first century, this was expressed by Stéphane Hessel in a way that stimulated great enthusiasm. As a French resistance fighter, Hessel endured torture in the Nazi concentration camps. Having gone on to help draft the United Nations Universal Declaration of

Human Rights and campaign for human rights thereafter, in 2010 he published the pamphlet *Time for Outrage*, which sold more than four million copies. His pamphlet urged everybody to be outraged at the existing situation in which the power of money had never been so great, selfish and shameless (Hessel, 2011: 22). 'The immense gap between the very poor and the very rich', he noted, 'never ceases to expand' (Hessel, 2011: 27). He called for peaceful resistance to this power of money, 'taking advantage of modern means of communication' (Hessel, 2011: 29). Socialists such as Hessel believe that without widespread outrage the required substantial change is likely to falter owing to indifference or resistance.

Having earlier sympathized with the communists, by the late twentieth century Hessel had come to favour a democratic approach and joined the French Socialist Party. Although he was thus broadly a social democrat, arguments for ordinary people to unite and act for themselves have also come from other sections of the socialist tradition. Indeed, such arguments were voiced in the early years of the socialist movement by Flora Tristan. Working-class people, she argued in 1843, needed to unify by each making small regular payments that would enable them to 'create a huge union to assert their unity!' By thus giving themselves strength, she went on, the working class 'will be able to make itself heard, to demand from the bourgeois gentlemen its right to work and organize' (Tristan, 2007: 59). By taking the initiative themselves, the working class would be able to gain representation and make demands on the state.

Other arguments for workers to act for themselves come from Marxists, including Rosa Luxemburg, who wrote *The Mass Strike* in 1906 after studying strike activity in Russia during the late nineteenth and early twentieth centuries, especially in the failed Russian revolution of 1905. The mass strike, she argued, represented the most likely situation in which workers would, spontaneously, become politically aware and active. The mass strike could not be described in abstract terms as a phenomenon to be triggered by a decision of the party (Luxemburg, 1986: 18–22). Instances of mass strike often did not result from planning, and even when there was some sort of political organization, the strikes soon escalated out of the control of the organizers. In each case, the strikes erupted or escalated when the workers themselves responded in this way to their conditions (Luxemburg, 1986: 23–45). This in turn would prepare them to unite and act for themselves in bringing down the capitalist order. It is only at that point, according to Luxemburg (1986: 46–56), that the party should provide leadership and direction. The economic struggle of the workers for better conditions would feed into a growing political campaign against the state which upholds the capitalist economy. Luxemburg argued that her theory would apply not just to Russia but to other countries in Europe, including Germany, when the appropriate conditions emerged.

Luxemburg thus focused her attention on workers. Some other socialists who likewise argue that people need to do considerably more than simply be led have stressed the importance of people in their other social roles. As will be seen in the next chapter, for example, Cole in his early guild socialist period considered the role of consumer to be particularly important. More than sixty years later, in 1985, Ernesto Laclau and Chantal Mouffe presented their influential argument that there were in fact many groups of oppressed people in contemporary capitalist societies, and that socialists need to recognize this situation rather than focus on workers in their class. More recently, Mouffe (2018: 60–1) has once again emphasized the necessity for the construction of a people around a radical project which addresses the various forms of subordination, exploitation and discrimination. This would be achieved by means of hegemonic politics to counter the existing hegemony. This building of counter-hegemony to achieve substantial and lasting social change has been considered an important task by a tradition of socialist thinkers beginning with Gramsci.

Countering hegemony

Gramsci was jailed by Mussolini in 1928. The law, the prosecutor demanded, 'must stop this brain from functioning for 20 years' (Jones, 2006: 24). The demand was unsuccessful. In the notebooks Gramsci produced in his cell before he died in 1937 – written in an opaque style, not least to avoid the attention of the jailors and censors – one can detect his argument that counter-hegemony should be developed to confront the hegemony of the existing dominant class. Each class, he argued, had its own organic intellectuals who consciously worked on behalf of their movement. Revolutionary intellectuals of the working class would emerge, leading to a situation in which the dominant class and its state would lose the consent of the masses and resort to coercion to retain control. The revolutionaries would have enough support to establish the new hegemonic movement, producing arguments that would appeal to other classes and groups, such as peasants and traditional intellectuals. The people would thus not need to be constantly led, but instead would adopt or consent to a revolutionary attitude and associate themselves with the goals of the movement (Gramsci, 1971: 196–202). The state, according to Gramsci (1971: 263), amounts to hegemony protected by the armour of coercion. The development of the new movement was necessary to challenge the hegemony of the existing order, which would be weakened gradually by adopting what he called a 'war of position', involving gradual consolidation of power and influence in society, rather than a 'war of manoeuvre', by which he meant direct action to overthrow the existing state. The revolutionaries would thus gain in strength while the hegemony of the existing order became exhausted as its legitimacy waned (Gramsci, 1971: 238–9). No longer consenting to that order, people would support the revolution.

Gramsci's work on consent and hegemony has roots in his writings of 1919–20, which had an associationalist element. 'The socialist state', he suggested, 'already exists potentially in the institutions of social life characteristic of the exploited working class' (Gramsci, 1977: 374). Inspired by the work of the Turin workers' councils since the end of the 1914–18 war, he argued that a new form of democratic government based on control of industry should replace the old parliamentary democracy, which was dominated by the capitalist classes and their allies. This 'proletarian revolution' would, he stressed, 'be a very long historical process' (Gramsci, 1977: 377). The bourgeois state would seek to break the revolutionary movement by means of force, and so, he went on, in a sentence that brings to mind his later war of position, the working class must 'be on its guard, it must maintain discipline in its revolutionary trenches, a discipline whose substance is patience, proletarian critical sense, and trust in its own forces and future' (Gramsci, 1977: 401). These workers' councils would not be hampered by old-fashioned trade unions which had no desire to undertake social and political change. To arrive at this situation, however, the Socialist Party would need initially to guide the struggle, leading to communism and thus the dictatorship of the proletariat. (Gramsci later lost faith in the Italian Socialist Party and thus formed the Communist Party.) The psychology of the workers would thereby be radically transformed, enabling them to gain the skill, capacity and inclination to govern themselves. Hence, there would be a combination of centralized power and autonomy in workers' and peasants' representative democracy.

Gramsci's conception of change envisaged people having a strong role in working towards their own future, even though there is a substantial element of vanguardism. Poulantzas was influenced by Gramsci's work, which he analysed critically. It was not, Poulantzas (1978: 258) argued, 'a question of a straight choice between frontal war of movement and war of position, because in Gramsci's use of the term, the latter always comprises encirclement of a fortress State'. It was necessary not just to take control of that state and either use or abolish representative democracy. Rather, socialists should aim to 'block the path of the State from outside through the construction of self-management "counter-powers" at the base – in short, to quarantine the State within its own domain and thus halt the spread of the disease' (Poulantzas, 1978: 262). To be fair to Gramsci, one can interpret his work on the Turin workers' councils as bearing similarities to what Poulantzas was thus suggesting. A clearer difference between the two thinkers was, however, that unlike Gramsci, who was concentrating on the workers, Poulantzas suggested the left must take up 'popular demands on fronts that used to be wrongly called "secondary" (women's struggles, the ecological movement, and so on)' (Poulantzas, 1978: 263–40). Poulantzas did not elaborate, but as we have seen in

Chapter 2 on freedom, equality and community, Laclau and Mouffe did explore this issue.

For Laclau and Mouffe, a new common sense needed to be constructed. This would change the identity of the groups seeking social and political change so that the demands of each are articulated equivalently. The 'free development of each', they suggested, quoting Marx and Engels from *The Communist Manifesto*, should thus 'be the condition for the free development of all' (Laclau and Mouffe, 1985: 183). Equivalence would mean that the interests of one such group would not be defended at the expense of others. To achieve this, the movement should be one that does 'not simply establish an "alliance" between given interests, but modifies the very identity of the forces engaging in that alliance' (Laclau and Mouffe, 1985: 184). The equivalence would thus be hegemonic, democratic and egalitarian.

At around the time that Laclau and Mouffe presented their argument, Robert Cox (1987: 7) extended the discussion of hegemony into the study of international relations, adapting and applying Gramsci's ideas accordingly. Cox argued that domestic and transnational class forces had combined with states and international institutions and organizations to form a world hegemonic order. 'This', he stressed, 'has nothing to do with specific manipulation of state policies or the actions of particular "actors" but with general under-standings about the tasks and limits of the state' (Cox, 1987: 6). The development of counter-hegemonic international forces was possible, but so far this had been thwarted by the existing hegemonic order by means of co-opting some of the opposing forces and dividing others. As there was no escape from some sort of world order, socialists would need to persevere in the international movement to build the counter-hegemony (Cox, 1987: 400–3). This leads us to the issue of the extent to which socialists should be internationalists.

The international question

Socialists often have internationalist aspirations. Indeed, prominent socialist parties of both the social democratic and

Marxist persuasions have usually considered it important to affiliate to international socialist organizations. In practice, however, they tend to operate predominantly within their own country, especially if there seems little prospect of achieving their goal internationally. Since the beginning of the socialist movement in the early nineteenth century, Laski suggested in his lecture *Socialism as Internationalism* in 1948, the principle of sovereignty rather than internationalist principles had, albeit not always consciously, been prioritized. Socialists had not been able to pass beyond the boundary line created by the inference of self-determination that 'a nation ought to be an organised community in which there is a government exercising the sovereign power' (Laski, 1949: 6). Socialists, he argued, needed to learn that 'the rhetoric of internationalism is not enough' (Laski, 1949: 16). As will be mentioned at the end of this chapter, Laski offered some innovative views on how to overcome the obstacles to fulfilment of internationalist aspirations.

The aspirations are clear to see in Marx and Engels' call at the end of *The Communist Manifesto* for workers of all countries to unite (Marx and Engels, 2002: 258). They are evident also in one of the most prominent contributions to Marxism in the twentieth century, Trotsky's theory of permanent revolution, which stressed that a revolution in Russia could only be successful if followed quickly by revolutions in the more advanced capitalist countries (Trotsky, 1977: 1029–30).

The French social democrat Jean Jaurès offered very different views of the importance of internationalism. In 1907, at a socialist congress in Stuttgart, he and his colleagues had passed a resolution, so far given only lukewarm support by existing governments, declaring 'the duty of the working classes of all countries to labor without a halt in favor of the cause of international arbitration' (Jaurès, 1908: 191). Claiming that this demand for arbitration was 'a new departure in our International Socialistic world', he stressed that 'Socialism, per se, has always stood for peace and against strife between brother nations' (Jaurès, 1908: 191). Acknowledging that until very recently, socialists had tended to take the Marxist line that they needed to abolish the existing capitalist order, Jaurès advocated instead the following very different approach: 'There must be a just and wise regulation of the economical warfare between nations.' Socialists, he went on, 'can aid in this good cause by teaching that the bettering of the condition of the working classes should be placed before the desire for greater productive activity'. This, for him, was an idea that 'should be inculcated among all nations' (Jaurès 1908: 196). There would, moreover, be 'larger liberties to peoples who are the victims of old-time conquests' (Jaurès, 1908: 198).

Like Jaurès, the Austrian social democrat Julius Braunthal was committed to the internationalization of the social democratic movement. The intense rivalry between Marxism-Leninism and social democracy in the second half of the twentieth century can be appreciated if one refers to an article Braunthal wrote in 1949. Having generally considered that it would eventually move on from the worst of its rights violations, the social democrats had been cautiously sympathetic to the USSR, especially when Stalin became an ally against Nazism. After Stalin had begun to take control over Eastern Europe, however, some leading socialist parties in the west of the continent approved the Western alliance that would later that year become the North Atlantic Treaty Organization (NATO). As Braunthal (1949: 589) put it: 'The mere fact that the Socialist movements of Western Europe actually did accept an alliance with capitalist America against Communist Russia denotes a most significant change of attitude.' Although Marxists had envisaged 'a revolution which would transform the capitalist countries of Europe into a federation of free and equal Socialist states, inspired by the nations most advanced in the economic and cultural fields', the communist revolution had brought about the subjection of the people of Eastern Europe 'to the dictatorial control of the state which is economically and culturally most backward' (Braunthal, 1949: 590–1). Stalin's USSR was thus hardly internationalist.

Nevertheless, as John Schwarzmantel reminds us, other socialists have often accepted the nation state as one among other frameworks for action. He stresses that utilizing the nation state for socialist purposes 'does not preclude the awareness of international solidarity and the strengthening of international links, the traditional aspiration to create a supra-national community' (Schwarzmantel, 1991: 2–3). 'National identity and membership of a national community need not', he suggests, 'preclude other identities, operating at the sub-national level, the supra-national level, or (for example, with regard to class identifications) possibly at the cross- or trans-national level' (Schwarzmantel, 1991: 5). The idea of the nation state is thus compatible with the associationalist strand within the socialist tradition.

The compatibility of movements of national liberation with socialist internationalism was a theme in Mao's revolutionary theory. In 1938, in the climate of China's war against Japanese imperialism, he delivered a series of lectures titled 'On Protracted War'. Reminding his audience that the '450 million people of China constitute one quarter of the world's population', he suggested that if 'they overthrow Japanese imperialism and create a new China of freedom and equality, they will most certainly be making a tremendous contribution to the struggle for perpetual world peace' (Mao, 1965a: 150).

In his essay 'On New Democracy' two years later, by which time the war against Japan had become part of the Second World War, Mao wrote that this was the latest episode of imperialist domination. In the areas not controlled by Japan, furthermore, China was still largely feudal or semi-feudal rather than capitalist, and so the revolution needed to overthrow imperialism and feudalism in its first stage before embarking on the second. This second stage would be that of the proletarian, socialist revolution (Mao, 1965b: 341–3). Mao had begun to make this point the previous year in 'The Chinese Revolution and the Chinese Communist Party'. At the present stage the revolution was, he stressed 'obviously' not proletarian-socialist but rather a bourgeois-democratic revolution of a new type, or in other words a 'new democratic revolution' developing not only in China but also 'in all other colonial and semi-colonial countries'. This revolution was nevertheless 'part of the world proletarian-socialist revolution, for it resolutely opposes imperialism, i.e., international capitalism' (Mao, 1965c: 326–7). By 'part of', Mao (1965c: 327) meant that the new democratic stage was one of transition which 'clears the way for capitalism on the one hand and creates the prerequisites for socialism on the other'.

Mao argued in 'On New Democracy' that capitalism 'could not survive without relying on the colonies and semi-colonies'. Since the Bolshevik revolution of 1917, the situation was such that the new socialist state (the USSR) had 'proclaimed its readiness to give active support to the liberation movement of all colonies and semi-colonies.' (Mao, 1965b: 343). 'In this era,' he stressed, 'any revolution in a colony or semi-colony that is directed against imperialism, i.e., against the international bourgeoisie or international capitalism', was 'part of the new world revolution, the proletarian-socialist world revolution' (Mao, 1965b: 343–4). For Mao, the nationalist and internationalist elements of socialist liberation were thus intertwined. The sort of society he hoped to build in China will be discussed in the next chapter.

Later in the twentieth century, leaders of nationalist movements against Western domination, including those in Cuba, Angola, Mozambique and Vietnam, were drawn towards Marxism-Leninism, supported by the USSR and subsequently encouraged to become parts of the internationalist communist movement (Duncan, 1988–9). The movement was divided: Vietnam, for example, sometimes leant towards the USSR and at other times towards China (Leighton, 1978). Nevertheless, there was international solidarity in some form or another. More recently, as will be discussed in the next chapter, the Venezuelan socialism of Hugo Chávez in the early twenty-first century was underpinned by a new combination of nationalist and internationalist principles.

For socialist internationalist aspirations to be realized, innovation is required. Laski discussed this in *Socialism as Internationalism*. Federalist schemes, for example for a United States of Europe, did not, he insisted, solve the problem that a relatively wealthy nation state would face a lowering of standards of living if it gave up the power 'to safeguard itself against cheap labour, or against goods produced more cheaply than it is itself able to produce them, or the threat to its pattern of living involved in any right to free migration within some larger area than those with which we are now familiar' (Laski, 1949 11). Laski was thus addressing problems that continue to reappear seventy years later. There could not, he added, be a swift transition to world government. The idea that the great powers would surrender their sovereignty was simply illusory.

Socialists, according to Laski, needed to push the development of functional organization, rather than the usual territorial federation, examples being 'international air lines, international railways, international power supply'. They should devise 'joint planning in the production of particular commodities, or plans so made that there is specialised production of one commodity in one country which is related to specialised production of some other commodity in another' (Laski, 1949: 15). Such bilateral arrangements could be extended to multilateral ones. Socialism, he stressed, would be far more suitable than capitalism for the purposes of such planning. While the field for fruitful cooperation was immense, however, audacity and experimentalism were needed. Laski's summary was brief but nevertheless significant for its recognition of the very real problems for socialist internationalism and the need for innovative solutions. Given the amount of progress needed within states to reach a position where international socialist organization is viable, it is perhaps hardly surprising that the focus tends to be on planning within national boundaries. In the next chapter, several blueprints for a socialist society serve to illustrate the variety of such plans.

5
Blueprints for a Socialist Society

G.A. Cohen (2009: 57) suggests that 'the principal problem that faces the socialist ideal is that we do not know how to design the machinery that would make it run'. There have, nevertheless, been attempts to draw up what might be called blueprints for the design of a new socialist society. The ones summarized in the present chapter represent the theoretical span of socialism since the early years of the twentieth century. A bigger book would have extended the historical range back to the early socialist thinkers such as Charles Fourier and Robert Owen. The narrower selection offered here consists of examples that each build on the Marxist, associational and social democratic theories that emerged and developed in the formative decades of the previous century.

Cole's guild socialism

In the associationalist tradition, the British guild socialists of the early twentieth century argued that workers in industry should control production collectively with significant autonomy from the state. Some guild socialists, such as S.G. Hobson and Ramiro de Maeztu, were authoritarian, believing that the guilds should control the workers and interpret the interests of consumers (Morgan, 2007). G.D.H.

Cole took guild socialism in a more democratic direction, arguing that the general will resided in the general machinery of the society and community and was expressed in different ways through geographical and functional associations such as in local government and guild councils, respectively (Lamb, 2005; Stears, 1998). He focused mainly on associations for workers performing functions in industry.

In *Self-Government in Industry*, published four months before the Russian Bolshevik revolution of October 1917, Cole argued for greater political democracy in the UK in conjunction with industrial democracy administered through a system of national guilds. The workers themselves, Cole argued, 'should have an ever-increasing measure of power and responsibility in control'. Capitalist supremacy could, he went on, 'be overthrown only by a system of industrial democracy in which the workers control industry in conjunction with a democratised state' (Cole, 1917: 4).

In 1919, in a new introduction to *The World of Labour*, first published in 1913, Cole urged the British Labour Party to be constructive. Rather than make its programme attractive to the bourgeoisie, the uniting of hand workers and brain workers in the party and the broader movement would involve functional democracy. As he put it: 'The application of the principle of democratic self-government, not merely to political organization, but to every sphere of social activity – to every social function of the community – is the vital concept of the new age' (Cole, 1928: xxi). The Bolshevik revolution had shown British workers that social and political change could happen, but Cole saw the need to adapt to the existing circumstances, thus making programmes for change achievable in the short term.

In 1920, in *Guild Socialism Restated*, Cole argued that the Bolshevik revolution 'produced everywhere a very powerful effect on the minds of the workers, and the knowledge of it, mingling in their consciousness with the other factors, created on their part a disposition far more ready for change' (Cole, 1980: 22–3). In his view, nevertheless, neither the British nor the American labour movement was presently strong enough to prevail by means of direct revolutionary action given the strength of capitalist society it faced. Hence, unless unforeseen circumstances such as those of October 1917 were to arise, Russian methods could not 'be applied either to the British or to the American situation' (Cole, 1980: 188).

Cole acknowledged that his scheme was revolutionary, but not in the sense of the Bolshevik revolution. In 1920, when Lenin (1966: 233) denounced guild socialism as 'pedantic rubbish', Cole published *Guild Socialism Restated* as an alternative to Bolshevism suitable to British conditions and political culture. He advocated 'encroachment', or 'encroaching control' (Cole, 1980: 196). The driving force would be the organized working class in industry, and he considered, optimistically, that the first stage of the gradual but nevertheless revolutionary process had already begun. British workers were changing their trade unions from negative organizations which reacted to and restricted capitalist exploitation to positive ones campaigning for greater goals (Cole, 1980: 20–5). The next stage would be the gradual process of taking over roles in the workshops. Functions or purposes performed by representatives of the capitalist class would, slowly but surely, pass to those of the working class. With the transference of rights and of responsibility for purposes would come the transference of economic power to workers and consumers (Cole, 1980: 32–3, 196–8).

Cole wrote *Guild Socialism Restated* with the tenets of freedom, community and equality in mind. In the first chapter, titled 'The Demand for Freedom', the goal of deepening democracy was also emphasized. To achieve this goal, he insisted, 'we must abolish class distinctions by doing away with the huge inequalities of wealth and economic power on which they depend' (Cole, 1980: 16). His blueprint was for an extensive system of self-governance. 'Only a community which is self-governing in this complete sense, over the whole length and breadth of its activities,' he argued, 'can hope to call out what is best in its members, or to give them that maximum opportunity for personal and social self-expression which is requisite to real freedom' (Cole, 1980: 13).

Cole's extensive institutional design comprised four major forms of organization, each having subdivisions. The industrial or economic guilds would each have representatives in the Industrial Guilds Congress, which would be the successor to the Trades Union Congress, and its local and regional counterparts (Cole, 1980: 69). Consumers would be represented in organizations of the cooperative movement, which would provide opportunities for self-government, and in what Cole called 'Collective Utility Councils', which would take over economic functions of the local authorities at several levels, including the wards, villages, towns and regions. At the different levels, there would be consultation between producers and consumers (Cole, 1980: 89–93). Turning to what Cole called the 'civic services', there would be guilds for each such service such as health and education. In the educational system, for example, 'teachers will possess a self-governing status fully equivalent to that of the economic workers' (Cole, 1980: 101) in their guilds. The civic service guilds would, like the workers' and consumers' guilds, have a national level and 'institutions responsible for education at all its stages – from primary school to University' (Cole, 1980: 103). Alongside and 'enter[ing] into close and constant relation' with the civic service guilds would be local health and cultural councils 'elected by all the citizens to express the civic point of view' (Cole, 1980: 108).

Together these organizations would contribute to the communal organization and spirit of society. The role of the state would be reduced to coordinating the activities of the functional organizations. Even this role would eventually wither away as the organizations grew accustomed to coordinating their activities and relations through elected representatives of their members in the wards of the communal body, or commune, of a city, town or region. The ward representatives would contribute directly to the decision-making of the commune itself (Cole, 1980: 117–38). Hence, workers in their trade unions would lead but not dominate the development of the new democratic system.

As we have already observed, by 1929 Cole had begun to think in social democratic terms. Conceding that guild socialism was impractical, he never, however, entirely abandoned this associational project, considering it as something to be aspired to. Indeed, during the Second World War he indicated that the functional democracy of guild socialism might be implemented if the future peace brought about a suitable environment (Cole, 1943: 30–3). In the short term, however, he considered that socialists should have far less grandiose objectives, as would C.A.R. Crosland in the 1950s.

Crosland's social democracy

In *The Future of Socialism*, Crosland (1956: 30, 462–82) insisted that nationalization was unnecessary for effective social control as the modernization and regulation of the economy could serve this purpose. Nationalization should be employed only where it could reduce inefficiency in industry. A new, mixed economy combining nationalized and private ownership could generate growth, the benefits of which could be distributed equitably. This, he observed, was already starting to happen as the old form of capitalism was giving way to an interventionist state, providing social welfare and full employment. To win elections, all parties now had to be sensitive to public attitudes (Crosland, 1956: 26–9).

To continue this course, increase the equitable distribution of wealth and, more importantly for Crosland, bring about broader social equality, class division would need to be overcome. Class was particularly entrenched as a feature of society in the UK. Unlike Marxists, whose conception of class distinguished between owners of the means of production, on the one hand, and workers hired for a wage, on the other, Crosland (1956: 169–89) saw class as a broader phenomenon involving all things that led to some people having greater power and being considered superior to others.

Class, according to Crosland (1956: 188), thus had both objective and subjective aspects which contributed to social inequality. The subjective aspect was the individual and collective feeling that people held about their class positions. This could lead to antagonism and resentment. The objective aspect was that of wide gaps among sections of the populace determined by factors such as income, power and style of life. These gaps tended to become more pronounced as the different sections avoided uninhibited intercourse between one another. Crosland (1956: 190–217) argued that reducing inequality would help avoid the antagonism and resentment and bring about greater social justice. The latter would allow people opportunities to realize their potential and flourish; receive awards for work which served important functions and contributed to national prosperity; experience a more even distribution of power; and receive appropriate rewards for work involving risk, responsibility and burden. It would also reduce social waste because children would no longer be segregated in education on the basis of class. Adults would subsequently achieve positions in society on the basis of merit rather than nepotism, favouritism and inherited property.

How much equality there should be in society was, for Crosland, an unknown quantity, and necessarily so 'unless one subscribes to the vulgar fallacy that some ideal society can be said to exist, of which blueprints can be drawn, and which will be ushered in as soon as certain specific reforms have been achieved' (Crosland, 1956: 216). Nevertheless, the view he expressed of what the future of socialism should look like can itself be considered as a blueprint in terms of an early design of the requirements for the better society to be achieved. 'We stand, in Britain,' he predicted, 'on the threshold of mass abundance' (Crosland, 1956: 515). This would allow comprehensive education to replace the existing system which divided children, thus contributing to the demise of the class system. The principle of the comprehensive school should be propagated, and resources spent on raising the standards of secondary modern education, thus weakening the prestige distinction between schools in the existing system (Crosland, 1956: 518).

Abundance would mean that instead of focusing on equality in terms of 'fair shares of austerity', the aim should be the plentiful diffusion of consumer goods. The motive should not be to foster the motive of personal gain, but rather 'to allow the working class at last to share the material ease and comforts which have for too long been the prerogative of a privileged few' (Crosland, 1956: 518). To fund this diffusion there would be an increase in property owned by the community funded by contributions of the wealthy in the form of various taxes such as death duty and rates on the larger estates. There would also be a capital gains tax and 'severe action against tax avoidance by the richer classes'

(Crosland, 1956: 519). Large increases in income tax should, on the other hand, be avoided.

Greater social expenditure would contribute to equality. Poorer families would thus gain benefits in fields such as education, health and housing. These benefits would be of a standard comparable to those enjoyed at present by means of private purchase by the wealthy. Every citizen should also have the freedom to enjoy leisure, art, culture and other such things that 'contribute to the varied fabric of a full private life' (Crosland, 1956: 520).

In industry, the trade unions would have far greater responsibility. The interests of the unions should extend to 'all major economic questions affecting an industry' (Crosland, 1956: 519). This would mean greatly enhancing worker participation and industrial democracy, thus transferring significant industrial power.

Other actions required to help bring about social equality would include intolerance of discrimination on the basis of sex and sexuality and the reduction of restrictions on abortion, divorce and censorship. People would thus feel liberated. Freedom and equality would thus each be features of the new order (Crosland, 1956: 521–4).

Had Crosland's blueprint been developed and implemented successfully, it would indeed have brought about a major, fundamental social transformation. There were reasons for optimism in the UK in the 1950s and 1960s. However, in the 1970s, those who benefited most from capitalism began to show greater interest in the ideas of thinkers such as F.A. Hayek and the libertarian Robert Nozick, and to organize accordingly. The Thatcher and Reagan governments in the UK and USA were determined to roll back the state insofar as it challenged vested interests. This set an example for other countries and inequality widened. Social democratic and labour parties grew timid in their responses. In the twenty-first century, even Crosland's prediction of capitalist stability proved to be inaccurate, and the aftermath to the financial crash of 2008 was felt most strongly by the working class as austerity policies were imposed in response. Crosland's blueprint began to look wildly optimistic. Meanwhile, very different socialist projects had been attempted in other parts of the world.

Mboya's African socialism

African socialism, according to its leaders and theorists, built on the continent's traditional societies. In Chapter 2, we looked briefly at Julius Nyerere's project in Tanzania, which eventually proved to be economically disastrous. Here we will examine the work of another African socialist theorist of note, Tom Mboya of Kenya.

As a leading trade unionist, Mboya was active in the struggle for Kenyan independence from the UK. He won a seat in the legislative council in the late 1950s and helped found the Kenya African National Union (KANU) in 1960, becoming a minister in the coalition government which negotiated independence three years later, whereupon he became minister for economic planning and development (Goldsworthy, 1982).

In the article 'African Socialism' of 1963 – the year of independence – Mboya insisted that socialism in his own continent was unique. From his pan-African perspective, he declared support for Kwame Nkrumah's goal of establishing African socialism in Ghana. Pan-Africanism as a movement was, for him, based on the experience of colonialism, which fostered a brotherhood with a sense of common destiny. He expressed a strong belief 'that in the field of economic relations we can similarly be guided by the traditional presence of socialist ideas and attitudes in the African mental make-up' (Mboya, 1963: 17). Those who considered themselves Marxists should, he suggested, start to think for themselves. Even many of those who did declare themselves to be African socialists should recognize that their thought processes were steeped in foreign thought processes and their actions detrimental to African brotherhood. African socialists should fight against the intellectual imperialism of neocolonialism and thus gain economic independence (Mboya, 1963: 18).

This did not, he stressed, mean that African socialism was fundamentally different from other forms of socialism. The tenets of socialism were universal. The point was that those tenets were formulated in different ways by socialists in different parts of the world. The human being was considered by Western socialists to be a social animal, meaning that 'every member of a society has certain obligations to the society in which he finds himself and conversely, every society has certain responsibilities towards its members' (Mboya, 1963: 18). Western socialists perceived society as organic, its members thus being interdependent. Hence, it was unnatural for a group of humans to control land, capital, skills and other things that enabled it to prosper at the expense of others in the society. Society should be organized around equal sacrifice, equal opportunity and individual freedom, with the state regulating economic life and controlling the vital means of production and distribution (Mboya, 1963: 18–19). This emphasis on equality and freedom ran alongside a view of community that respected African norms and values. African socialism, as Mboya (1963: 18) saw it, adopted traditional codes of conduct that preserved the dignity and security of all African people, irrespective of social position, such as universal charity, and also the thought processes which considered people as ends rather than means.

Although sympathetic to many aspects of Western socialism, Mboya was no social democrat. He played a major role in the KANU one-party state in Kenya. Nevertheless, as he stressed to the KANU conference in 1965, he rejected communist ideology. 'The time has come', he declared, 'for those who go around using the phrase African Socialism as a cloak to introduce some alien doctrine to cease their song' (Mboya, 1965: 14). Communism was another form of colonialism. Kenyan African socialism should, therefore, follow the path of non-alignment in international relations.

There was a practical reason for Mboya's stance. Whilst rejecting Western colonialism, he advised that Kenya should develop new relationships with the Western countries and to continue to trade with them, always on guard to ensure that colonial dominance would not be renewed in other ways (Mboya, 1965: 13). Declaring that the African frame of mind closely resembled that of the Western socialist tradition, he nevertheless suggested that: 'In Africa the belief that "we are all sons (and daughters) of the soil" has exercised tremendous influence on our social, economic and political relationships.' From this common relation to the soil arose 'the logic and practice of equality' and 'a belief in the practice of communal ownership of the vital means of life' (Mboya, 1963: 18). This tempered the acquisitiveness which afflicted Western society. Laziness was not tolerated; industriousness was encouraged. Poverty existed but the social economic and cultural gap was narrow. In Africa, unlike in Western society, wealth did not necessarily entail power. All things considered, Africa had a human environment that was naturally conducive to socialism.

Mboya argued that African socialist thinking should guide transformation and development in newly independent Kenya with its largely agricultural populace and economy. He offered his blueprint accordingly, the priority being to expand and modernize agricultural and related production. This would require better farming methods and investment 'in irrigation, flood control, land reclamation, provision of agricultural machinery and equipment, research and in improving communication' (Mboya, 1963: 18). Agricultural research and training would be crucial to progress and success, allowing Kenya to move rapidly away from European domination. Expected outcomes would include more employment and food for the people as the rural economy was developed. The strategy would also produce a surplus for export which in turn would enable the country to generate the foreign exchange to import materials necessary for the diversification of the Kenyan economy, including industrialization.

Mboya advocated agricultural cooperatives as the best means of efficient farming. In trade and industry, there would be direct participation by the people in ownership, direction and management – on which he did not elaborate. The government would provide funds to train local entrepreneurs, establish a development bank, provide loans to stimulate private investment and make social legislation to enable people to enjoy security and employment. The government would also invest in hospitals, education, transport infrastructure and training in the field of health (Mboya, 1963: 19).

Mboya's blueprint may seem unremarkable, adopting measures previously employed in various combinations by different sorts of socialists around the world. What is significant is the African socialist ethos which underpinned the project. Intellectuals, businessmen and the trade unions would, according to Mboya, each have important roles. Intellectuals, whatever their field, should pick up the thread of the African socialist tradition and be active in politics. Businessmen should contribute to the establishment of industrial democracy and economic planning, developing business ethics suitable to the situation. Meanwhile, the trade unions should enjoy freedom of association to defend their members but also use their power for the good of all society rather than just their leaders and members, thus accelerating the process of capital formation and laying the foundations of industrial development (Mboya, 1963: 19).

Despite Mboya's efforts to unite and modernize his country, it remained riven by deep and violent tribal hostilities and the Kenyan left itself was divided. Furthermore, having advocated a mixed economy, he watched his popularity among Kenyan radical socialists wane. He made many enemies and was assassinated in 1969. Kenya sided with the West in the Cold War. The tribal divisions did not heal and Kenyan aspirations for African socialism faded away.

Mao's socialism for China

A very different socialist project was developed by Mao for revolutionary change in twentieth-century China, as mentioned in the previous chapter. Developed over many years before the communists took power in the revolution of 1949, Mao's project stressed that theory should be neither dictated by elites nor abstracted from everyday life. Theoretical precepts based on education and wider knowledge would be integrated with the everyday experiences and existence of the masses, drawing simultaneously on Marxist and Leninist theory and the particular conditions of China (Deutscher, 1977: 192–7).

In his speech 'Problems of War and Strategy' in 1938, Mao stressed that China was neither democratic nor independent but, rather, semi-colonial and semi-feudal. Under feudal oppression and subjugated by imperialism, particularly by the occupying Japanese, there was in China no parliament and no legal right to organize for workers' strikes. There would, hence, be nothing to gain from undertaking a long period of legal struggle before launching insurrection, armed force and war, first in the countryside and then in the big cities (Mao, 1965d: 219–23).

The influence of Marx and Lenin is clear in Mao's 'On New Democracy' of 1940, as is the belief developed over two decades that China must take a course based on its history, geography, demographics and international potential. As Chinese capitalism was not at an advanced stage, the peasantry would be crucial to the struggle for communism. Mao (1965b: 339–40) expressed this in terms of seeking truth from facts: 'The only yardstick of truth is the revolutionary practice of millions of people.' He declared that his Communist Party had been struggling for many years to build a new society and state for the Chinese nation. This required political, economic and cultural revolution.

As Mao (1965b: 340) argued in a statement which summarized his blueprint, not only did he and his revolutionaries 'want to change a China that is politically oppressed and economically exploited into a China that is politically free and economically prosperous, we also want to change the China which is being kept ignorant and backward under the sway of the old culture into an enlightened and progressive China under the sway of a new culture'. That culture must, he continued, reflect the politics and economics of its society, and specifically the new politics and economics to be introduced by the Chinese communists (Mao, 1965b: 340–1).

As was discussed briefly in the previous chapter, Mao considered the revolution he was leading to consist of two main stages. He argued that the communists had already embarked on the first, democratic stage (Mao, 1965b: 341–4). The Western bourgeois type of democracy, introduced in Sun Yat-sen's Chinese revolution of 1911, had thus begun but not completed the transition to a new democracy. The latter had nevertheless become part of the proletarian-socialist world revolution which began in Russia in October 1917. In the colonies and semi-colonies of the capitalist powers, new democratic revolutions would likewise be led by the proletariat in the drive to progress through the development of capitalism and towards the socialist society. As part of this process, Mao (1965b: 347) suggested, 'the proletariat, the peasantry, the intelligentsia and other sections of the petty bourgeoisie in China have become a mighty independent political force under the leadership of the Chinese Communist Party'.

The first stage of revolution would 'result in the establishment of a new-democratic society under the joint dictatorship of all the revolutionary classes of China headed by the Chinese proletariat' (Mao, 1965b: 347). At this point, the national bourgeoisie, which opposed domination from both abroad and within their country, could play a role in overcoming imperialism and the regional warlords but could, Mao (1965b: 348–9) cautioned, change sides. The second stage of the revolution would establish a socialist society in China and constitute an important part of the world revolution (Mao, 1965b: 347).

The politics of the new democracy would involve two related systems. First, there would be 'a system of people's congresses, from the national people's congress down to the provincial, county, district and township people's congresses, with all levels electing their respective governmental bodies'. Second, for proper representation of each revolutionary class and the expression of the will of the people, 'a system of really universal and equal suffrage, irrespective of sex, creed, property or education, must be introduced'. Mao (1965b: 352) referred, without elaboration, to the combination of these two systems as 'democratic centralism' – a notion originally formulated before the October revolution of 1917 by the Russian Social Democratic Workers' Party (RSDWP) which would later become the Communist Party.

In revolutionary Russia, democratic centralism referred to organizational cohesion and Western-type democratic procedures within the RSDWP. The dire economic situation in the early years of the revolution, along with internal and international opposition to the Bolsheviks, led the organizational aspect to be strengthened while the democratic aspects of election and accountability waned as nomination and strict censorship took the place of election and free speech. Strict party discipline and the binding authority of decisions by the higher organs upon lower organs and members predominated. This authoritarian conception of democratic centralism became a central feature of communist parties and states (Waller, 1981: 4–8, 12). Nevertheless, it was interpreted in various ways. Seeking to combine Marxism and Leninism with actual conditions, the Chinese communists insisted that the views of the mass peasantry could not be ignored. The party would summarize and systemize the views of the masses and then take the results back to the masses. This approach became known as the mass line (Waller, 1981: 91–5).

'Because of the leadership of the proletariat,' Mao (1965b: 378) reiterated, although the socialist revolution could only be achieved after the present new-democratic one, 'the politics, the economy and the culture of New Democracy all contain an element of socialism'. This decisive element could enable the new culture to be built. Marxism-Leninism would play 'the guiding role', Mao (1965b: 378) continued, 'and we should work hard both to disseminate socialism and communism throughout the working class and to educate the peasantry and other sections of the people in socialism properly and step by step'.

Turning to the economy, Mao said that although capitalist private property in general would not be confiscated, the state would own, operate and administer the big banks and the major industrial and commercial enterprises, including railways and airlines. Capital would thus be regulated to prevent it from dominating the livelihood of the people. The Marxist influence becomes very clear at the point where Mao advocated the confiscation of land from the landlords for distribution among the peasants. This could, Mao suggested, be the end of feudalism but not yet socialism. It would mean the 'equalization of landownership' in the form of private ownership by the peasants. In largely underdeveloped, agricultural China, with its history of imperialist exploitation and defensive war against Japan, feudalism would thus need to be followed by this new stage before the introduction of socialism. This can be seen as a form of historical materialism suited specifically to China. 'In general,' Mao (1965b: 353) suggested, 'socialist agriculture will not be established at this stage, though various types of co-operative enterprises developed on the basis of "land to the tiller" will contain elements of socialism.' Faced with opposition from international capitalism, China would, furthermore, need the assistance of the USSR and the proletarians in the capitalist countries in the drive towards socialism.

Mao led his communists to victory over both Japan and the Kuomintang, now led by Sun Yat-sen's successor, Chiang Kai-shek, which sought to impose a capitalist-oriented dictatorship. Although the communists took power in 1949, Mao considered China still to be in the new-democratic, rather than socialist, stage of revolution. The country, he declared in his speech 'Be a True Revolutionary' of 1950, was still undergoing new-democratic reforms. 'In the future,' he went on, 'it will enter the new era of socialism unhurriedly and with proper arrangements when our economy and culture are flourishing, when conditions are ripe and when the transition has been fully considered and endorsed by the whole nation' (Mao, 1965e: 39).

The attempted transition was disastrous. The Great Leap Forward of the late 1950s and early 1960s prioritized rapid collectivist industrialization and neglected vital agricultural development. Tens of millions died (Bernstein, 2006). The Cultural Revolution of the 1960s and 1970s involved up to another million deaths, mass suppression and chaos as Mao encouraged constant challenge from the grassroots to the central authorities (Walder and Yang Su, 2003). After Mao's death in 1976, the Chinese communists began to replace arbitrary rule with constitutional procedures to maintain and develop their authoritarian interpretation of Marxist socialism (Peng, 2012). The project continues today, which cannot be said of Yugoslav socialist self-management, which was based on a rather different interpretation of democratic centralism.

Kardelj and Yugoslav socialist self-management

Mao's mass line theory interpreted democratic centralism in a way that combined central direction with participation from the grassroots. The Yugoslav communists devised a far more formal, structured democratic centralist framework for participation, leading to their expulsion from Stalin's communist bloc in 1948. The Yugoslav leader, Tito, presided over the renaming of the Communist Party four years later as the League of Communists of Yugoslavia. The League promised to withdraw from direct involvement in government and administration and instead provide guidance over a system of self-managed institutions. Over the next two decades, the League gave greater autonomy to its branches in the constituent republics of Yugoslavia but, nevertheless, in the 1970s still retained unrivalled power throughout the country's political, social and economic, and security structures. The League began to interpret democratic centralism as decentralization of administration combined with centralized planning mechanisms. The administration would be performed by self-managed organizations while the central role would be particularly strong in the economic sphere (Waller, 1981: 102–6).

Yugoslavia had emerged from the Second World War against Germany and the other Axis countries in the hands of the united communist partisans of the constituent republics. The economy of the new communist state was predominantly agricultural and undeveloped. In the 1950s, Edward Kardelj, who had fought as a Slovene partisan and was now a senior figure in both the League of Communists and thus the government, was a leading theorist of self-management. 'We do not believe', he said in his article 'Evolution in Jugoslavia' of 1956, 'that there exist universal political blueprints valid for all countries or even for all stages of Jugoslavia's own development' (Kardelj, 1956: 582).

Kardelj insisted in the article that, having begun from a backward condition after the war, the Yugoslav economy could only develop on socialist lines gradually, and in peaceful cooperation with countries having different social and political systems. In the early years of the revolution following the war, moreover, it had been necessary to have high degrees of centralization and concentration of power. This had, however, begun to produce bureaucracy and inertia, failed to generate incentives and stifled creative effort and initiative. Kardelj saw the need for a blueprint to suit Yugoslavia at its stage of economic and political development having progressed through its initial post-revolutionary period. Progress had indeed already been started over the previous few years on the development of a system of administrative internal control that would make excessive centralization superfluous. Although he did not use the term 'self-management' in the article, the measures he championed in it would come to be known as such. 'This control was', he elaborated, 'based on the economic and social interests of the workers' collectives in the various enterprises, of the individual workers, and of the basic social communities, namely the municipalities and districts' (Kardelj, 1956: 483–4). For this system to improve production, individual workers, the collectives in which they worked and their local areas would need to have stakes in the results and both material and moral incentives. This had already resulted in the replacement of a bulky centralized administrative machinery with 'economic incentives and the free cooperation and association of enterprises on a functional basis' (Kardelj, 1956: 484). This was self-management, to which market socialism bears affinities. Large individual enterprises were given management control over parts of the national wealth, their employees making production, hiring, and marketing decisions. The role of the central economic plan was simply, by means of a legal framework, to set the goals, lay down the essentials of the policy and outline the general lines of distribution of production and income.

There would, according to Kardelj, also be significant decentralization in the political system, with democratic forms of government and integration growing out of the new economic system. The basic units of this structure would be the workers' councils. Elected by the workers of each enterprise, the councils would in turn make sure the economic functions of the decentralized organizations worked in the general interest of society, operating within the requirements of the overall national plan. The self-governing committees of the communes (municipalities and districts) and the parliaments of the Yugoslav federation and constituent republics would make decisions on the more general issues (Kardelj, 1956: 584–92).

Kardelj died in 1979, and the following year a collection of his writings, *Tito and the Socialist Revolution of Yugoslavia*, was published. Although frankly hagiographic in the tradition of communist literature on leaders, the book included some clear statements by Kardelj of the origins and aims of the Yugoslav blueprint, including his address to the central committee of the League in 1967 and an article he published in 1972.

Kardelj's article of 1972 considered why the self-management model was developed. Following the attack on the Yugoslav communists Stalin had delivered in 1948 with the aim of discrediting the leadership and subjugating the party and thus Yugoslavia itself, Tito had chosen to resist, leading to the Soviet–Yugoslav split. The main decisive lesson of the experience was, Kardelj (1980: 94) declared, 'our even greater understanding of the significance and real danger of progressive and revolutionary centralism degenerating into technocratic centralism and bureaucratic willfullness'. Stalin's attack had thus opened the way 'to the revolutionary practice and theoretical conception of workers' and social – or as we then called it, people's – self-management'. The decision to introduce and implement socialist workers' and social self-management, sanctioned by Tito, had, Kardelj (1980: 97) went on, 'been decisive in the development of our socialist society and especially its liberation from the dangers of the various deformations typical of bureaucratic centralism'.

Tito, Kardelj (1980: 52) suggested in the speech of 1967, had stressed the following key points. First, 'self-management is not just the right and privilege of the working man but also his constant responsibility'. Second, enterprises, institutions and publics services were the concern not only of 'their individual working collectives but of the entire community'. Third, each working collective must 'actively join its forces with those of other working collectives and in full consciousness undertake cooperation, division of labour and integration generally'. Fourth, 'self-management frees neither the political nor economic planning organs of the state from their responsibility for the situation in the country'. These points help illustrate the democratic centralist nature of the self-management blueprint.

The Yugoslav version of democratic centralism with its element of self-management brought about a considerable narrowing of inequality between the Yugoslav republics (Waller, 1981: 107). Nevertheless, the remaining

inequalities caused dissatisfaction and a level of state intervention acceptable to all the republics could not be found
(Marković, 2011: 125–6). When in the 1960s the League
began to allow rival candidates (but not from other parties),
the centralist aspect was weakened, inequalities between the
republics widened and some candidates began to express
nationalist sentiments (Waller, 1981: 107–8). After Tito's
death in 1980, these sentiments escalated. By the early 1990s,
the entire federal structure had collapsed as Yugoslavia broke
up in a series of wars between the republics (Critchley, 1993).
Self-management was a casualty of this collapse.

Chávez's Bolivarian socialism

Venezuelan socialism, led by Hugo Chávez, had what can
perhaps be described as an evolutionary blueprint in action
following the formation of the Revolutionary Bolivarian
Movement (MBR) in 1982. Renaming his movement
MBR-200 the following year to mark the two hundredth
anniversary of the birth of Simón Bolívar, whose South
American revolution against Spanish imperialism was driven
by the ideals of liberty and equality (Gonzalez, 2014: 33–9),
Chávez gradually constructed an organizational and institutional framework to put his ideas into practice. The
movement became the Movement of the Fifth Republic
Movement (MVR) in 1997 in preparation for elections the
following year, in which Chávez was elected president of
Venezuela. The MVR operated as a political party which,
with its allies, dominated parliament after the 2005 elections.
It eventually merged with some of its coalition partners and
formed the United Socialist Party of Venezuela in 2007.
Although not himself a political thinker, Chávez built his
movement and planned its Bolivarian revolution on quite
a coherent theoretical basis, envisaging a republic based on
Bolívar's ideas. Chávez's evolving blueprint can be pieced
together from a series of interviews he conducted in 2004
with the Cuban activist Aleida Guevara (eldest daughter of
the revolutionary leader Che Guevara) and correspondence in
2006 with the US Marxist economist Michael A. Lebowitz.

Clearly influenced by Lebowitz, Chávez made an innovative intellectual contribution to socialism.

Chávez summarized the basis of his 'Bolivarian ideology' as follows: 'Bolívar is not just a man, Bolívar is a concept. More than just a theory, Bolívar is a complex set of ideas related to politics, society, and justice' (Chávez and Guevara, 2005: 11). Chávez's theory and movement had both nationalist and internationalist elements – the latter being the argument for regional, Latin American integration and unity. The nationalist element was for a truly independent Venezuela to build a new society based on a system of egalitarianism and social justice.

As national independence was from contemporary imperialism, the nationalist and internationalist elements were combined. As Chávez put it to Guevara: 'In the 20th century, Venezuela became a country rich with oil and resources of every description, but it was also full of poverty – a rich country full of poor people' (Chávez and Guevara, 2005: 9). Chávez's goal was to overcome the international exploitation of Venezuela, thus allowing resources, including oil, to be used for the common good, starting with the elimination of poverty.

Chávez said that upon leaving prison in March 1994 after serving two years for a failed coup attempt, he decided that the revolution would be peaceful, by means of elections. Although, as he conceded, at that point his peaceful method lacked clear definition, later that year the MBR-200 contested mayoral and gubernatorial elections. Over the next few years, members of the movement travelled the country to spread their message, resulting in Chávez's electoral success of 1998 and the subsequent referendum which gained approval for a constitutional assembly. The assembly introduced a new constitution in 1999, replacing the Venezuelan Fourth Republic with the Fifth (Chávez and Guevara, 2005: 18–22). One immediate problem the republic faced was the low price of oil as the result of high production, which, Chávez suggested, was an intentional US strategy, followed dutifully by previous Venezuelan governments. To counter this he cut back oil production, meaning lower expenditure in proportion to income.

A major government programme, Plan Bolívar 2000, was launched in 1999, beginning with a scheme in which soldiers participated in a civil–military effort focused, Chávez stressed, 'on the poorest sectors, repairing schools, building local markets and providing food' (Chávez and Guevara, 2005: 24). The success of the plan led him to build a new army, the officers being contemporaries and comrades who shared the Bolivarian ideology. The aim was to build an army of civic-minded soldiers committed to social justice and social welfare programmes for the needy (Chávez and Guevara, 2005: 26–31).

The social welfare programmes became a key feature of the evolving Plan Bolívar, the objectives of which Chávez outlined in utilitarian terms. 'The perfect form of government', he suggested to Guevara, 'is that which guarantees the greatest degree of happiness for its people,' this being the objective or central aim of his movement and government. As Venezuela was 'in the midst of massive social need', he went on, the creation of the government was, 'effectively, a political and constituent-led revolution' (Chávez and Guevara, 2005: 33). He described how the new constitution was drafted and introduced in an atmosphere in which all were invited to discuss their issues. Initially overwhelmed by the pressure of different groups demanding rights and justice, he recollected, 'Plan Bolívar would place the armed forces at the disposal of a state that had previously been an obstacle and a brake on society' (Chávez and Guevara, 2005: 34). The implementation of the plan extended to previously neglected areas including health care, education and housing. Not wanting help from the IMF or similar organizations, and unable to rely on revenue from Venezuelan oil, the plan proceeded with sparse resources. A new newspaper, *El Correo del Presidente* (The President's Mail), was 'designed mainly to inform the public of what we were doing, of the gravity of the situation we had inherited and to ask for their patience' (Chávez and Guevara, 2005: 36). International support for the plan was sought, securing cuts to oil production. 'By the end of 1999,' Chávez recalled, 'oil was at $16 a barrel, enabling us to increase social spending despite our external debt' (Chávez and Guevara, 2005: 36). The plan continued to develop, notwithstanding both the pressure of huge demand and a devastating avalanche which hit Vargas state. A people's bank was set up and by 2000 foreign investment began to increase, unemployment had begun to fall and Venezuela entered a period of economic stability. At presidential, parliamentary and gubernatorial elections, the movement gained increased majorities, enabling Chávez to, as he put it, 'change the Supreme Court and the National Electoral Council' (Chávez and Guevara, 2005: 39). In 2000, the movement had a two-thirds majority in the national assembly. By 2002, the privatization of the oil industry had been reversed (Chávez and Guevara, 2005: 45). In other sectors of the economy, new state-owned companies were set up. The state and public sector, which included many new cooperatives, concentrated particularly closely on the distribution of foodstuffs. The project benefited from new revenue from the sale of oil, notably to Cuba, which had previously been blocked due to US pressure and rulings (Chávez and Guevara, 2005: 60–1).

Although in 2002 Chávez was removed from power by means of a coup d'état, the following year he regained the presidency in elections that international observers deemed fair. In the period before his next presidential electoral victory four years later, he worked with Lebowitz to provide a theoretical basis for twenty-first-century socialism.

Lebowitz has published two papers he wrote as an adviser to the Venezuelan government, along with discussion of Chávez's comments on them. In the first paper, Lebowitz discussed three categories of productive relations, each based on a form of property relations. These were capitalist, cooperative and statist productive relations. He discussed ways of using these categories in order to design non-exploitative productive relations. While capitalist firms could be subordinated though measures such as taxation and nationalization, a new form of capitalist productive relations not based on exploitation would be impossible to achieve. Hence, capitalist enterprises would need to be transformed into statist or cooperative ones in the socialist society (Lebowitz, 2014: 2–9).

After reading the paper, Chávez contacted Lebowitz (2014: 9) to emphasize that as it was organic, with all its aspects interconnected, capitalism needed to be transcended rather than transformed by means of fundamental reconstruction. Lebowitz's second paper investigated how this task should be undertaken. Lebowitz (2014: 10–11) sought to address the following question: 'how can you make any real changes if you have to change all relations – and you cannot change them all simultaneously?' The process of developing the new socialist society must be to subordinate all elements of capitalism to a logic centred on human beings. This in turn would proceed by 'by assembling the elements of a new dialectic of production–distribution–consumption'. Those elements, he went on, would be part of a new combination at the core of which are three characteristics: '(a) social ownership of the means of production which is a basis for (b) social production organized by workers in order to (c) satisfy communal needs and communal purposes' (Lebowitz, 2014: 11). Social ownership was not necessarily state ownership, or in other words ownership at the national level, but rather a democratic arrangement where communication of needs and purposes would help people function as producers and as members of society. The influence of Marx on Lebowitz's thought is clear in his comment that the relations of production would be cooperative, with people working in solidarity with one another, thus ending the alienation experienced in capitalist society. '[T]he free development of each' would, Lebowitz (2014: 12) suggested, quoting Marx, thereby 'be the condition for the free development of all'.

For Lebowitz, each of the three elements depended on the existence of the other two. The production–distribution–consumption complex was thus inseparable, the effects of each element being felt in the other two. Lebowitz acknowledged that Chávez read this theoretical paper and responded by interpreting the interrelated elements as the 'elementary triangle of socialism ... by setting out three points on his desk and explaining each side'. This, Lebowitz suggested, was an example of Chávez's 'unique ability to take complex theoretical concepts and to communicate these to the masses of viewers without a theoretical background' (Lebowitz, 2014: 18).

For Lebowitz (2014: 13), a major achievement of the Bolivarian Revolution was 'the creation of the Communal Councils, an essential cell of socialism for the twenty-first century'. People could, together, identify communal needs democratically and become aware of means to meet those needs. The councils could thus be considered in terms of a school of socialism.

After the Communal Council Law had been passed in Venezuela in April 2006, considerable investment in the councils led to their proliferation throughout the country, especially in underprivileged areas. Public works projects were designed and executed in the councils, which also solicited funding. The councils encouraged political participation in the communities, but also led to distrust of political and bureaucratic intervention from the centre, leading the government to temporarily limit their expansion and sideline their importance (Ellner, 2014: 90–1).

Contrary to Lebowitz's enthusiasm for the councils, Mike Gonzalez (2014: 114, 120) suggests that although they had been considered as key to the system of participatory democracy promised by Chávez, the law of April 2006 had subjected the councils to national leadership and given them a function of social intelligence which encouraged informing on fellow members of the community. Nevertheless Chávez was re-elected president in December, and in 2011, he considered the conditions appropriate to revitalize the communal councils (Ellner, 2014: 91). He was elected president once again in 2012.

By 2011, the Venezuelan economy had begun to decline. Chávez died in 2013 and his successor as president, Nicolás Maduro, tried to revive Plan Bolívar. Elected by a slim majority as the economy continued to weaken, Maduro faced increasing hostility at home and from abroad. He did initially manage to stimulate the proliferation of the communal councils (Ellner, 2014: 92). His government also, however, adopted authoritarian measures to retain control as the economy declined further and austerity grew. Whether Chávez, Maduro, the USA, the wider international capitalist world or a combination thereof was to blame, the Plan Bolívar blueprint had failed.

6
Conclusion

Having emerged in the early nineteenth century, socialism is still resonant today, not least in its influence on movements and ideas of a broader left. Since the 1990s, for example, theorists and activists operating under an anti-capitalist banner have challenged the global capitalist system. Capitalist hegemony suppressed opposition by making alternatives appear unrealistic and undesirable. A people divided and thus weakened by imaginary differences was a source of capitalist power. In response, the anti-capitalist movement appealed to many to whom conventional politics seemed futile (Callinicos, 2003). As the injustices of capitalism transcended the boundaries of sovereign states, the movement stressed the need to organize internationally, seeking to discredit transnational corporations and the international organizations which served their interests. Redistribution of wealth, it was hoped, could be achieved and environmental and ecological destruction averted to ensure something worthwhile remains to be distributed among people having the freedom to flourish without discrimination on grounds of class, sex, sexuality, race or ethnicity. As Susan George (2004) put it, if action begins to be taken in these respects, another world is possible.

Socialism can continue to provide the theoretical justification for anti-capitalism. The organized working class which is the lifeblood of socialism has, moreover, a potentially crucial role to play in overcoming international capitalism and its exploitative practices. Indeed, drawing on the ideas of Marx and Luxemburg, Steven Colatrella identified strikes by workers in various industries and countries after the global economic crisis of 2008, in response to austerity engineered for the defence of capitalist interests. Interpreting the state as 'a set of institutions and functions that are the residue of class struggles of the past', Colatrella argues that capital has reorganized the state in a way that diminishes institutions and functions on which the organized working class can have influence, and bolstered those that 'are closer in personnel, socialization and function to capitalist interests' (Colatrella, 2011: 83). For him, the WTO, the G20, World Bank and IMF had played significant roles in this process.

As Colatrella (2011: 87) discusses, in response to austerity, action was taken by 'a host of movements, organizations and protests, at times uniting in action a diversity of class actors'. At the spearhead, he insists, was working-class action, largely in the form of strikes. This soon evolved into a political crisis in a number of countries around the world, starting with contributions to the unrest in the Arab countries which attracted worldwide media attention. Organized workers recognized that the global governance institutions and organizations were key factors in bringing about austerity. Importantly, Colatrella (2011: 93) acknowledged: 'As in classical revolutionary situations, middle-class and professional protests merged with mass workers' strikes, leading to direct challenges to political authority.' In turn the capitalist class influenced state policies 'formulated, initiated and fostered by global governance'. Colatrella suggested that in the contemporary global economy, wherein workers in crucial industries and locations could have a significant impact upon the linking points between national and global economies, there was evidence of workers engaging in international solidarity. The capitalist system thus faced a 'political crisis' (Colatrella, 2011: 95). He stressed, nevertheless, that 'any polity is more complex and varied than the simplified accounts of any strictly class analysis suggest' (Colatrella, 2011: 103–4).

Concerned almost entirely with the crucial role of the organized working class in the struggle against international capitalism, Colatrella only mentioned the involvement of other groups and classes very briefly. An important point that socialists should, however, bear in mind is that the individuals, states and international institutions involved in the increasingly global institutional processes that defend the capitalist class do not target the working class alone as a source for exploitation. In some cases, it may be more productive to exploit women of various classes. Alternatively, by making some categories of human being into the Other, the capitalist class can maintain the myths of desirable lifestyles that preserve stability and continuity while exploiting and scapegoating marginalized groups. These practices are, furthermore, often institutionalized rather than consciously designed and implemented.

To help create a counter-hegemony, socialists need to look beyond the working class, acknowledge the chains of equivalence and convince people in other exploited, oppressed and scapegoated categories of two things. First, capitalism presents obstacles to the freedom of each to flourish. Second, such obstacles can be overcome by building an egalitarian society based on a democratic community in which people from the range of groups are heard and respected.

The creation of the new hegemony in the twenty-first century requires the willingness of socialists and other groups to work together within the anti-capitalist movement. Ecological problems, for example, which render traditional socialist reliance on economic growth outdated, may still be solvable by means of the amalgam of equality, freedom and community if the expertise of people and groups sympathetic to socialism is taken on board. To adapt to the requirements of this and other contemporary issues, socialists need to ask themselves a few questions. Can they, for example, campaign against capitalist exploitation and for equitable distribution in a spirit of community while not expecting to consume resources in ways once taken for granted? Can they devote more attention than has traditionally been the case to the non-class issues without weakening their commitment to the working class? If so, the socialist movement needs to adopt change but can still provide steering. Some recent, innovative work on the left helps indicate what socialism needs to do and the significance it retains.

Chantal Mouffe argues that, as groups on the far right today exploit both the weakness of neoliberalism and the demise of confidence in democracy by resorting to populist tactics, the left needs to develop its own populism. In the neoliberal decades, the democratic tenets of equality and social justice lost their appeal as possessive individualism became even more dominant than when C.B. Macpherson used the term in the 1960s. Having come to signify free elections, the defence of human rights, but no more, democracy morphed into post-democracy. Right-wing populism, framed as an attack on elites and a restoration of democracy, was really a strategy for the development of nationalistic and authoritarian forms of neoliberalism incorporating very restricted versions of democracy (Mouffe, 2018: 1–24). 'What is urgently needed', Mouffe (2018: 36) argues, 'is a left populist strategy aimed at the construction of "a people", combining the variety of democratic resistances against post-democracy in order to establish a more democratic hegemonic formation.' This 'people' would be formed from 'a collective will that results from the mobilization of common affects in defence of equality and social justice'. The people can thus be a community. By means of the construction of this people, she goes on, 'it will be possible to combat the xenophobic policies promoted by right-wing populism' (Mouffe, 2018: 6).

Socialists attracted to Mouffe's idea may need first to adopt a populist strategy within their own party to overcome opposition. Hilary Wainwright (2018: 13–21) argues that practical knowledge developed by people in cooperation with one another can become the transformative power which ensures that strategies for political hegemony are controlled democratically rather than taken over by elites which claim to know better than ordinary people what is good for them. A problem arises, however, if a leader gains mass support amongst their membership against resistant senior party figures, as was the case in the British Labour party under Jeremy Corbyn (Watts and Bale, 2019). This may bring division in a party rather than cooperation. To help minimize such division, socialism needs to reach beyond its traditional base of support within a party, which, if it is to avoid declining in size, will need to include members who have progressive beliefs wider than those with which it is traditionally associated. As Wainwright (2018: ix–x) suggests, a 'new politics from the left is in the making' with the potential to build a diverse movement 'to create an open, participatory, green and feminist form of socialism'. This will need to differ from traditional social democracy, which had little faith in the ability of ordinary people to participate in politics. Power as a transformative capacity will need to be gained by ordinary people in their everyday, cooperative interactions with one another. Through collective action in institutions such as trade unions and various community groups, people discover that they have the capacity to bring about change (Wainwright 2018: 18–21).

The arguments of Wainwright and Mouffe complement one another. If a left populism is to succeed, this could be by means of the power as transformative capacity that people can be encouraged to develop. Wainwright, however, places more emphasis on the extent to which the people can construct themselves, albeit in collaboration with a political party in parliament.

Offering ideas compatible with those of Mouffe and Wainwright, Leo Panitch and Sam Gindin (2018: 11) are concerned that the 'ideological delegitimation' of neoliberalism has presented the far right, 'with its ultra-nationalist, racist, sexist and homophobic overtones', with the space 'to capture popular frustrations with liberal democratic politics'. Nevertheless, they stress that this delegitimization 'has restored some credibility to the radical socialist case for transcending capitalism as necessary to realize the collective, democratic, egalitarian and ecological aspirations of humanity' (Panitch and Gindin, 2018: 11–12). For Panitch and Gindin (2018: 16), these ideas should be referred to as democratic socialism, retaining a clear distinction between it and social democracy. The social democratization of those now committed to transcending capitalism must, they insist, be avoided.

Mouffe, Wainwright, Panitch and Gindin are suggesting that socialism must recognize that people in the twenty-first century no longer accept being led by a paternalistic elite – communist or democratic. People can still be persuaded that community and equality are crucial to a fulfilling life but want to find their own ways to self-fulfilment. Emancipation and thus freedom are important to them, and any socialists wanting to succeed today need to recognize this. Axel Honneth sees it very clearly. For him, socialism developed around a belief in the relationship between three principles in conflict with one another in the capitalist economic order. These principles were liberty, equality and fraternity, which socialism reconciled in the term 'social freedom'. He summarizes this as follows:

> Human beings cannot realize their individual freedom in the matters most important to them on their own. The satisfaction of generally shared needs depends on intersubjective relationships that are only 'free' under certain normative conditions – the most important of which is the mutual sympathy found only in communities of solidarity. (Honneth, 2017: 27)

As Honneth suggests, a problem socialists face in trying to maintain the resonance of this notion of social freedom is that it tends to be associated with the economic conditions of the industrial revolution. Social and economic conditions are, of course, now very different to those of the nineteenth century in poor and richer countries. Hence, as Honneth (2017: 50) declares: 'Only if the original vision of social freedom can be articulated in a theory of society and history that lives up to contemporary reality will it be able to regain a piece of its earlier validity.'

Returning to Mouffe, she fully recognizes that a left populist project is unlikely to succeed if it harks back to yesterday's world. This raises again the point she and Laclau stressed in 1985: socialism needs to break free from its communist and social democratic traditions and actively engage in campaigns based on chains of equivalence between it and other social movements which oppose capitalism. Socialists can accept this point about chains of equivalence while still making clear that neither capitalist exploitation of the working class nor action in response by organized labour has gone away. Other movements seek to overcome oppression of groups, this being no more or less significant than the socialist aim of liberating the working class from exploitation. Those other movements could ally with socialism, thus enabling each to reach their own emancipations. Perhaps the other groups and movements should consider Oscar Wilde's opening words of his essay *The Soul of Man under Socialism* in 1891: 'The chief advantage that would result from the establishment of Socialism is, undoubtedly, the fact that Socialism would relieve us from that sordid necessity of living for others which, in the present condition of things, presses so hardly upon almost everybody. In fact, scarcely anyone at all escapes' (Wilde, 2001: 127).

A hegemonic project such as Mouffe's is necessary, however, if socialists are to do more than expose the harm that capitalism involves. There is recent evidence from Canada, Sweden, the USA and the UK that over time people will begin to lose tolerance of inequality when austerity bites too hard (Hicks et al., 2016). This could be a basis on which socialists can build. There is also recent evidence that people will align with political parties and movements when the concepts of left and right begin to appear relevant to their lives (Fortunato et al., 2016). Nevertheless, although Bernie Sanders came close to winning the contest for the Democratic Party's candidature in the 2016 presidential election in the USA, his support was largely a product of distrust of mainstream politicians (Dyck et al., 2018). If they are to retain and consolidate support, socialists need to build counter-hegemony from their place on the left in terms of equality, community and social freedom.

One thing socialists must do if their movement is to retain contemporary significance is devise policies to address the environmental disaster that is looming not least because of the policies of the right. Some socialists may go as far as John Sanbonmatsu (2007), for whom socialism needs to develop a new theory and practice of what he calls metahumanism to reconcile human emancipation with broader nature – the two being inseparable. Alternatively, socialists can turn to the early writings of Marx for inspiration. Marx insisted that humans produce and transform their own natural environment and their species in everyday life. Alec Loftus (2009: 160–1) suggests that Marx thus provides 'a wonderful springboard for a political ecology of the possible'.

As awareness of the gravity of the environmental crisis is growing, this could indeed be the seed of socialist counter-hegemony. Socialists need to accept that by producing and transforming the environment, humans have determined the nature of the biosphere and the condition of the planet's water, soil and other material, thus taking the world into the present epoch. Although sometimes called the Anthropocene, socialists also need to insist that 'Capitalocene' is a better title for this epoch, as the world has developed in the way it has in the several hundred years of capitalist dominance, during which time even non-capitalist parts of the world have had to work within a broader capitalist framework (Dolenec, 2019). As part of their counter-hegemony, socialists should seek to influence notions of justice immanent in international discourse on environmental issues. The objective of the Paris Agreement on Climate Change to limit the global temperature rise to 1.5 °C above the pre-industrial level is consistent with both the right to development that is central to international human rights law and the right to promote sustainable development already adopted by the United Nations Framework Convention on Climate Change (Gupta and Arts, 2018). The socialist combination of equality, community and social freedom should be promoted by socialists in discourse on the nature of justice in an international society which respects the need to control climate change.

Scientific and technological development can continue but with the aim of improving the standard of life of ordinary people equally in their communities, without worsening the environmental crisis. Technological development, however, raises another issue with which socialists need to engage. As mentioned in the Introduction, Tony Fitzpatrick (2003) saw the potential for developments in information technology to increase surveillance and exploitation in capitalist interests. With capitalist hegemony still in place, this situation seems unlikely to change. As developments in artificial intelligence (AI) proceed further, the deskilling of large sections of the populace of the richer capitalist countries could increase inequality within richer countries and between their skilled citizens and the millions of poor people elsewhere in the world, unless education enables all citizens to use technology for the benefit of society (Hodgson, 2003). This would require inroads into the processes upon which capitalism relies, based as it is on exploitation. As Illah Reza Nourbakhsh (2015: 24) put it, 'the pace of change in robotics is far outstripping the ability of regulators and lawmakers to keep up, especially as large corporations pour massive investments into secretive robotics projects that are nearly invisible to government regulators'. The best systems and robots will be available to the already wealthy and powerful, but also enhance the means of control of the already exploited. Demands that the new technology should only be available to people who have undergone the proper moral and ethical training count for little when the morals are shaped by the hegemonic culture that sustains the existing situation.

AI, robotics and cybertechnology can also be utilized constructively to enhance rather than diminish one's humanity if they increase the freedom people have as communal beings. Just one example would be the further development of technological devices used within the human body. If the counter-hegemony makes such development possible, then people may be able not only to emancipate themselves from capitalism but also to enjoy better lives thereafter. The problem is that at present their opponents in the capitalist system still hold the best cards. A long period of counter-hegemony building is needed if socialists are to mount a successful challenge.

References

Arblaster, A. (1984). *The Rise and Decline of Western Liberalism*. Oxford: Basil Blackwell.

Ball, T. and Dagger, R. (1999). *Political Ideologies and the Democratic Ideal*, third edition. New York: Longman.

Beech, M. and Hickson, K. (2007). *Labour's Thinkers: The Intellectual Roots of Labour from Tawney to Gordon Brown*. London: Tauris.

Beecher, J. (2013). 'Early European Socialism'. In G. Klosko (ed.), *The Oxford Handbook of the History of Political Philosophy*. Oxford: Oxford University Press, pp. 369–92.

Beecher, J. (2019). 'French Socialism and Communism'. In J. Diamanti, A. Pendakis and I. Szeman (eds), *The Bloomsbury Companion to Marx*. London: Bloomsbury, pp. 218–29.

Berki, R.N. (1975). *Socialism*. London: J.M. Dent and Sons.

Bernstein, E. (1993). *The Preconditions of Socialism*. Cambridge: Cambridge University Press.

Bernstein, T.P. (2006). 'Mao Zedong and the Famine of 1959–1960: A Study in Wilfulness', *The China Quarterly*, 186: 421–45.

Bevir, M. (2011). *The Making of British Socialism*. Princeton, NJ: Princeton University Press.

Blair, T. (1994). *Socialism*. London: Fabian Society.

Block, F. (1977). 'The Ruling Class Does Not Rule: Notes on the Marxist Theory of the State', *Socialist Revolution*, 7 (3): 6–28.

Braunthal, J. (1949). 'The Rebirth of Social Democracy', *Foreign Affairs*, 27 (4): 586–600.

Brezinski, H. (1990). 'Private Agriculture in the GDR: Limitations of Orthodox Socialist Agricultural Policy', *Soviet Studies*, 42 (3): 535–53.

Brisbane, A. (1840). *Social Destiny of Man; Or Association and Reorganization of Industry*. Philadelphia: C.F. Stollmeyer.

Burbach, R. (2014). 'The Radical Left's Turbulent Transitions'. In S. Ellner (ed.), *Latin America's Radical Left: Challenges and Complexities of Political Power in the Twenty-First Century*. Lanham, MD: Rowman and Littlefield, pp. 27–42.

Burnham, D. and Lamb, P. (2019). *The First Marx: A Philosophical Introduction*. London: Bloomsbury.

Buzby, A.L. (2010). 'Socialism'. In M. Bevir (ed.), *Encyclopedia of Political Theory*, Vol. 3. Thousand Oaks, CA: Sage, 1295–301.

Caldwell, B. (1997). 'Hayek and Socialism', *Journal of Economic Literature*, 35 (4): 1856–90.

Callinicos, A. (2003). *An Anti-Capitalist Manifesto*. Cambridge: Polity.

Cárdenas, R.R. (2014). 'A Nation Divided: Venezuela's Uncertain Future', *World Affairs*, 176 (6): 47–54.

Chávez, H. and Guevara, A. (2005). *Chávez, Venezuela and the New Latin America: An Interview with Hugo Chávez*. Melbourne: Ocean Press.

Cohen, G.A. (2000). *If You're an Egalitarian, How Come You're So Rich?* Cambridge, MA: Harvard University Press.

Cohen, G.A. (2009). *Why Not Socialism?* Princeton, NJ: Princeton University Press.

Colatrella, S. (2011). 'In Our Hands is Placed a Power: Austerity, Worldwide Strike Wave, and the Crisis of Global Governance', *Socialism and Democracy*, 25 (3): 82–106.

Cole, G.D.H. (1914–15). 'Conflicting Social Obligations', *Proceedings of the Aristotelian Society*, 15: 140–59.

Cole, G.D.H. (1917). *Self-Government in Industry*. London: G. Bell and Sons Ltd.

Cole, G.D.H. (1923). *Social Theory*, third edition. London: Methuen.

Cole, G.D.H. (1925–6). 'Loyalties', *Proceedings of the Aristotelian Society*, 26: 151–70.

Cole, G.D.H. (1928). *The World of Labour*, fourth edition. London: Macmillan.

Cole, G.D.H. (1929). *The Next Ten Years in British Social and Economic Policy*. London: Macmillan.

Cole, G.D.H. (1943). 'Plan for Living'. In G.D.H. Cole et al., *Plan for Britain*. London: Labour Book Service, pp. 1–33.

Cole, G.D.H. (1980). *Guild Socialism Restated*. New Brunswick, NJ: Transaction.

Connolly, W.E. (1977). 'A Note on Freedom under Socialism', *Political Theory*, 5 (4): 461–72.

Cox, R.W. (1987). *Production, Power and World Order: Social Forces and World Order: Social Forces in the Making of History*. New York: Columbia University Press.

Crick, B. (1987). *Socialism*. Milton Keynes: Open University Press.

Critchley, W.H. (1993). 'The Failure of Federalism in Yugoslavia', *International Journal*, 18 (3): 434–47.

Crosland, C.A.R. (1956). *The Future of Socialism*. London: Jonathan Cape.

Darlington, R. (2013). 'Syndicalism and Strikes, Leadership and Influence: Britain, Ireland, France, Italy, Spain and the United States', *International Labor and Working-Class History*, 83: 37–53.

Davis, A. (1982). 'Women, Race and Class: An Activist Perspective', *Women's Studies Quarterly*, 10 (4): 5–9.

Deutscher, I. (1953). 'Dogma and Reality in Stalin's "Economic Problems"', *Soviet Studies*, 4 (4): 349–63.

Deutscher, I. (1977). 'Maoism: Its Origins and Outlook'. In R. Blackburn (ed.), *Revolution and Class Struggle: A Reader in Marxist Politics*. Glasgow: Fontana/Collins, pp. 191–223.

Djilas, M. (1957). *The New Class: An Analysis of the Communist System*. London: Thames and Hudson.

Dolenec, D. (2019). 'Ecology and Environmentalism'. In J. Diamanti, A. Pendakis and I. Szeman (eds), *The Bloomsbury Companion to Marx*. London: Bloomsbury, pp. 541–7.

Duncan, R. (1988–9). 'Ideology and Nationalism in Attracting Third World Leaders to Communism: Trends and Issues in the Late Twentieth Century', *World Affairs*, 151 (3): 105–16.

Dyck, J.J., Pearson-Merkowitz, S. and Coates, M. (2018). 'Primary Distrust: Political Distrust and Support for the Insurgent Candidacies of Donald Trump and Bernie Sanders in the 2016 Primary', *PS: Political Science and Politics*, 51 (2): 351–7.

Ellner, S. (2014). 'Social and Political Diversity and the Democratic Road to Change in Venezuela'. In S. Ellner (ed.), *Latin America's Radical Left: Challenges and Complexities of Political Power in the Twenty-First Century*. Lanham, MD: Rowman and Littlefield, pp. 79–102.

Engels, F. (1968). 'Speech at the Graveside of Karl Marx'. In K. Marx and F. Engels, *Selected Works in One Volume*. London: Lawrence and Wishart, pp. 429–30.

Engels, F. (1976). *Anti-Dühring (Herr Eugen Dühring's Revolution in Science)*. Peking: Foreign Language Press.

Fabian Society (1884). *Why Are the Many Poor?* London: Geo. Standring.

Fabian Society (1890). *What Socialism Is.* London: Fabian Society.

Fitzpatrick, T. (2003). *After the New Social Democracy: Social Welfare for the Twenty-First Century.* Manchester: Manchester University Press.

Fortunato, D., Stevenson, R.T. and Vonnahme, G. (2016). 'Context and Political Knowledge: Explaining Cross-National Variation in Left–Right Knowledge', *The Journal of Politics*, 78 (4): 1211–28.

Fourier, C. (1996). *The Theory of the Four Movements.* Cambridge: Cambridge University Press.

Fraser, I. and Wilde, L. (2011). *The Marx Dictionary.* London: Continuum.

Fraser, N. (1995). 'From Redistribution to Recognition? Dilemmas of Justice in a "Post-Socialist" Age', *New Left Review*, 212: 68–93.

Freeden, M. (2003). *Ideology: A Very Short Introduction.* Oxford: Oxford University Press.

Fukuyama, F. (1992). *The End of History and the Last Man.* London: Hamish Hamilton.

Geary, D. (2003). 'The Second International: Socialism and Social Democracy'. In T. Ball and R. Bellamy (eds), *The Cambridge History of Twentieth-Century Political Thought.* Cambridge: Cambridge University Press, pp. 219–38.

George, S. (2004). *Another World is Possible If....* London: Verso.

Giddens, A. (1998). *The Third Way: The Renewal of Social Democracy.* Cambridge: Polity.

Giddens, A. (2000). *The Third Way and Its Critics.* Cambridge: Polity.

Goldsworthy, D. (1982). 'Ethnicity and Leadership in Africa: The "Untypical" Case of Tom Mboya', *The Journal of Modern African Studies*, 20 (1): 107–26.

Gonzalez, M. (2014). *Hugo Chávez: Socialist for the Twenty-First Century.* London: Pluto Press.

Gorbachev, M. (1988). *Perestroika: New Thinking for Our Country and the World.* London: Fontana/Collins.

Gorz, A. (1994). *Capitalism, Socialism, Ecology.* London: Verso.

Gramsci, A. (1971). *Selections from Prison Notebooks.* London: Lawrence and Wishart.

Gramsci, A. (1977). 'The Turin Workers' Councils'. In R. Blackburn (ed.), *Revolution and Class Struggle: A Reader in Marxist Politics.* Glasgow: Fontana/Collins, pp. 374–409.

Gupta, J. and Arts, K. (2018). 'Achieving the 1.5 °C Objective: Just

Implementation Through a Right to (Sustainable) Development Approach', *International Environmental Agreements*, 18 (1): 11–28.

Haug, F. (1991). 'The End of Socialism in Europe: A New Challenge for Socialist Feminism', *Feminist Review*, 39 (1): 37–48.

Hess, M. (1964). 'The Philosophy of the Act'. In A. Fried and R. Sanders (eds), *Socialist Thought: A Documentary History*. New York: Anchor Books, pp. 249–75.

Hessel, S. (2011). *Time for Outrage!* London: Quartet Books.

Heywood, A. (2012). *Political Ideologies: An Introduction*. Houndmills: Palgrave Macmillan.

Hicks, T., Jacobs, A.M. and Matthews, J.S. (2016). 'Inequality and Electoral Accountability: Class-Biased Economic Voting in Comparative Perspective', *The Journal of Politics*, 78 (4): 1076–93.

Hirst, P. (1988). 'Associational Socialism in a Pluralist State', *Journal of Law and Society*, 15 (1): 139–50.

Hodgson, G.M. (2003). 'Capitalism. Complexity, and Inequality', *Journal of Economic Issues*, 37 (2): 471–8.

Holmes, L. (2009). *Communism: A Very Short Introduction*. Oxford: Oxford University Press.

Honneth, A. (2017). *The Idea of Socialism*. Cambridge: Polity.

Jaurès, J. (1908). 'International Arbitration from a Socialistic Point of View', *The North American Review*, 188 (633): 188–98.

Jennings, J. (1991). 'Syndicalism and the French Revolution', *Journal of Contemporary History*, 26 (1): 71–96.

Johnston, D. (2010). 'Liberalism'. In M. Bevir (ed.), *Encyclopedia of Political Theory*, Vol. 2. Thousand Oaks, CA: Sage, pp. 795–802.

Jones, S. (2006). *Antonio Gramsci*. London: Routledge.

Kagarlitsky, B. (2000). *The Return of Radicalism*. London: Pluto Press.

Kardeji, E. (1956). 'Evolution in Jugoslavia', *Foreign Affairs*, 34 (4): 580–602.

Kardelj, E. (1980). *Tito and the Socialist Revolution of Yugoslavia*. Belgrade: STP.

Karyotis, G. and Rüdig, W. (2018). 'The Three Waves of Anti-Austerity Protest in Greece, 2010–2015', *Political Studies Review*, 16 (2): 158–69.

Kautsky, K. (1936). *The Economic Doctrines of Karl Marx*: London: A. & C. Black Ltd.

Laborde, C. (2000). *Pluralist Thought and the State in Britain and France, 1900–25*. Basingstoke: Macmillan.

Laclau, E. and Mouffe, C. (1985). *Hegemony and Socialist Strategy: Toward a Radical Democratic Politics*. London: Verso.

Lamb, P. (2004). *Harold Laski: Problems of Democracy, the Sovereign State, and International Society*. New York: Palgrave Macmillan.

Lamb, P. (2005). 'G.D.H. Cole on the General Will: A Socialist Reflects on Rousseau', *European Journal of Political Theory*, 4 (3): 283–300.

Lamb, P. (2015). *Marx and Engels' Communist Manifesto: A Reader's Guide*. London: Bloomsbury.

Lamb, P. (2016). *Historical Dictionary of Socialism*, third edition. Lanham, MD: Rowman and Littlefield.

Lange, O. (1964). 'On the Economic Theory of Socialism'. In O. Lange and F.M. Taylor, *On the Economic Theory of Socialism*. New York: McGraw Hill, pp. 55–129.

Laski, H.J. (1921). *The Foundations of Sovereignty and Other Essays*. London: George Allen and Unwin.

Laski, H.J. (1925). *A Grammar of Politics*. London: George Allen and Unwin.

Laski, H.J. (1930). *Liberty in the Modern State*: London: Faber and Faber.

Laski, H.J. (1938). *A Grammar of Politics*, fourth edition. London: George Allen and Unwin.

Laski, H.J. (1949). *Socialism as Internationalism*. London: Fabian Publications and Victor Gollancz.

Lassalle, F. (1990). 'Open Letter to the National Labor Association of Germany'. In F. Mecklenburg and M. Stassen (eds), *German Essays on Socialism in the Nineteenth Century*. New York: Continuum, pp. 79–102.

Lebowitz, M.A. (2014). 'Proposing a Path to Socialism: Two Papers for Hugo Chávez', *Monthly Review*, 65 (10): 1–19.

Leighton, M. (1978). 'Vietnam and the Sino-Soviet Rivalry', *Asian Affairs*, 6 (1): 1–31.

Lenin, V.I. (1947). *What is to be Done?* Moscow: Progress Publishers.

Lenin, V.I. (1966). 'Report on the International Situation and the Fundamental Tasks of the Communist International'. In V.I. Lenin, *Collected Works, Volume 31*: Moscow: Progress Publishers, pp. 215–34.

Lenin, V.I. (1976). *The State and Revolution*. Peking: Foreign Languages Press.

Lewis, J. (1983). 'Conceptualising Equality for Women'. In T. Atkinson et al., *Socialism in a Cold Climate*. London: Unwin, pp. 102–23.

Li, M. (2013). 'The 21st Century: Is There an Alternative (to Socialism)?', *Science and Society*, 77 (1): 10–43.

Lichtheim, G. (1975). *A Short History of Socialism*. Glasgow: Fontana/Collins.

Loftus, A. (2009). 'The *Theses of Feuerbach* as a Political Ecology of the Possible', *Area*, 41 (2): 157–66.

Luxemburg, R. (1986). *The Mass Strike*. London: Bookmarks.

Macpherson, C.B. (1962). *The Political Theory of Possessive Individualism*. Oxford: Oxford University Press.

Mao Tse-Tung (1965a). 'On Protracted War'. In *Selected Works of Mao Tse-Tung, Volume Two*. Peking: Foreign Languages Press, pp. 113–94.

Mao Tse-Tung (1965b). 'On New Democracy'. In *Selected Works of Mao Tse-Tung, Volume Two*. Peking: Foreign Languages Press, pp. 339–84.

Mao Tse-Tung (1965c). 'The Chinese Revolution and the Chinese Communist Party'. In *Selected Works of Mao Tse-Tung, Volume Two*. Peking: Foreign Languages Press, pp. 305–34.

Mao Tse-Tung (1965d). 'Problems of War and Strategy'. In *Selected Works of Mao Tse-Tung, Volume Two*. Peking: Foreign Languages Press, pp. 219–35.

Mao Tse-Tung (1965e). 'Be a True Revolutionary'. In *Selected Works of Mao Tse-Tung, Volume Five*. Peking: Foreign Languages Press, pp. 37–40.

Marcos, Subcomandante (2004). 'The Hourglass of the Zapatistas'. In T. Mertes (ed.), *A Movement of Movements: Is Another World Really Possible?* London: Verso, pp. 3–15.

Maréchal, S. (1964). 'Manifesto of the Equals'. In A. Fried and R. Sanders (eds), *Socialist Thought: A Documentary History*. New York: Anchor Books, pp. 51–5.

Marković, G. (2011). 'Workers' Councils in Yugoslavia: Successes and Failures', *Socialism and Democracy*, 25 (3): 107–29.

Marshall, P. (1993), *Demanding the Impossible: A History of Anarchism*, London: Fontana.

Marx, K. (1968a). 'Theses on Feuerbach'. In K. Marx and F. Engels, *Selected Works in One Volume*. London: Lawrence and Wishart, pp. 28–30.

Marx, K. (1968b). 'Critique of the Gotha Programme'. In K. Marx and F. Engels, *Selected Works in One Volume*. London: Lawrence and Wishart, pp. 311–31.

Marx, K. (1968c). 'Preface to *A Contribution to the Critique of Political Economy*'. In K. Marx and F. Engels, *Selected Works in One Volume*. London: Lawrence and Wishart, pp. 180–4.

Marx, K. (1968d). 'The Eighteenth Brumaire of Louis Bonaparte'.

In K. Marx and F. Engels, *Selected Works in One Volume*. London: Lawrence and Wishart, pp. 94–179.

Marx, K. (1968e). 'The Civil War in France'. In K. Marx and F. Engels, *Selected Works in One Volume*. London: Lawrence and Wishart, pp. 248–309.

Marx, K. (1976). *Capital, Volume One*. Harmondsworth: Penguin.

Marx, K. (1977). *Economic and Philosophic Manuscripts of 1844*. Moscow: Progress Publishers.

Marx, K. and Engels, F. (1974). *The German Ideology*, second edition. London: Lawrence and Wishart.

Marx, K. and Engels F. (1996). 'Manifesto of the Communist Party'. In T. Carver (ed.), *Marx: Later Political Writings*. Cambridge: Cambridge University Press, pp. 1–30.

Marx, K. and Engels, F. (2002). *The Communist Manifesto*. London: Penguin.

Mboya, T. (1963). 'African Socialism', *Transition*, 8 (March): 17–19.

Mboya, T. (1965). 'Kanu Non-Alignment', *Africa Today*, 12 (4): 12–14.

McKanan, D. (2010). 'The Implicit Religion of Radicalism: Socialist Party Theology, 1900–1934', *Journal of the American Academy of Religion*, 78 (3): 750–89.

McLellan, D. (2006). *Karl Marx: A Biography*, fourth edition. Basingstoke: Palgrave Macmillan.

Miliband, R. (1969). *The State in Capitalist Society*. London: Weidenfeld and Nicolson.

Miliband, R. (1983). *Class Power and State Power*. London: Verso and NLB.

Miliband, R. (1994). *Socialism for a Sceptical Age*. Cambridge: Polity.

Miller, D. (1990). *Market, State and Community: Theoretical Foundations of Market Socialism*. Oxford: Oxford University Press.

Mitchell, J. (1975). 'Women's Liberation, Marxism and the Socialist Family'. In B. Parekh (ed.), *The Concept of Socialism*. London: Croom Helm, pp. 221–30.

Morais, L. and Saad-Filho, A. (2011). 'Brazil beyond Lula: Forging Ahead or Pausing for Breath?', *Latin American Perspectives*, 38 (2): 31–44.

Morgan, K. (2007). 'British Guild Socialists and the Exemplar of the Panama Canal', *History of Political Thought*, 28 (1): 120–57.

Mouffe, C. (1993). *The Return of the Political*. London: Verso.

Mouffe, C. (2018). *For a Left Populism*. London: Verso.

Neocleous, M. (1997). *Fascism*. Buckingham: Open University Press.

Newman, M. (2005). *Socialism: A Very Short Introduction*. Oxford: Oxford University Press.

Nourbakhsh, I.R. (2015). 'The Coming Robot Dystopia: All Too Inhuman', *Foreign Affairs*, 94 (4): 23–8.

Nove, A. (1991). *The Economics of Feasible Socialism Revisited*, second edition. London: HarperCollins.

Nyerere, J. (1974). 'From Uhuru to Ujamaa', *Africa Today*, 21 (3): 3–8.

Nyerere, J. (1997). 'One-Party Government', *Transition*, No. 75/76, The Anniversary Issue: Selections from Transition, 1961–1976: 156–61.

Owen, R. (1991). *A New View of Society and Other Writings*. London: Penguin.

Panitch, L. and Gindin, S. (2018). *The Socialist Challenge Today: SYRIZA, Sanders, Corbyn*. London: Merlin Press.

Parekh, B. (1982). *Marx's Theory of Ideology*. London: Croom Helm.

Pelling, H.M. (1956). *America and the British Left: From Bright to Bevan*. New York: New York University Press.

Peng, A.(C.) (2012). 'Sinicized Marxist Constitutionalism: Its Emergence, Contents and Implications'. In M. Johnson (ed.), *The Legacy of Marxism: Contemporary Challenges, Conflicts and Developments*. London: Continuum, pp. 151–69.

Peterson, L. (1981). 'The One Big Union in International Perspective: Revolutionary Industrial Unionism 1900–1925', *Labour/Le Travail*, 7: 41–66.

Phelps, C. (2007). 'A Neglected Document on Socialism and Sex', *Journal of the History of Sexuality*, 16 (1): 1–13.

Poulantzas, N. (1969). 'The Problems of the Capitalist State', *New Left Review*, 58: 67–78.

Poulantzas, N. (1973). *Political Power and Social Classes*. London: NLB.

Poulantzas, N. (1978). *State, Power, Socialism*. London: NLB.

Rawls, J. (1999). *A Theory of Justice*, revised edition. Oxford: Oxford University Press.

Roemer, J.E. (1992). 'The Morality and Efficiency of Market Socialism', *Ethics*, 102 (3): 448–64.

Rousseau, J.-J. (1993a). 'A Discourse on the Origin of Inequality'. In J.-J. Rousseau, *The Social Contract and Discourses*. London: Everyman, pp. 31–126.

Rousseau, J.-J. (1993b). 'The Social Contract'. In J.-J. Rousseau. *The Social Contract and Discourses*. London: Everyman, pp. 179–309.

Rowbotham, S. (2013). 'The Women's Movement and Organising for Socialism'. In S. Rowbotham, L. Segal and H. Wainwright, *Beyond the Fragments: Feminism and the Making of Socialism*. London: Merlin, pp. 125–240.

Sacks, K.B. (1989). 'Towards a Unified Theory of Class, Race and Gender', *American Ethnologist*, 16 (3): 534–50.

Sanbonmatsu, J. (2007). 'The Subject of Freedom at the End of History: Socialism beyond Humanism', *The American Journal of Economics and Sociology*, 66 (1): 217–36.

Sarkar, S, (1991). 'The Future of Socialism – which Socialism?', *Alternatives*, 16 (3): 367–76.

Sassoon, D. (2014). *One Hundred Years of Socialism: The West European Left in the Twentieth Century*, second edition. London: I.B. Tauris.

Saunders. P. (1995). *Capitalism: A Social Audit*. Buckingham: Open University Press.

Schwarzmantel, J. (1991). *Socialism and the Idea of the Nation*. New York: Harvester Wheatsheaf.

Schweickart, D. (1998). 'Market Socialism: A Defense'. In B. Ollman (ed.), *Market Socialism: The Debate among Socialists*. New York: Routledge, pp. 7–22.

Seldon, A. (2005). *Blair*, second edition. London: Free Press.

Seliger, M. (1976). *Ideology and Politics*. London: George Allen and Unwin.

Service, R. (2000). *Lenin: A Biography*. London: Pan.

Service, R. (2010). *Trotsky: A Biography*. London: Pan.

Shaw, G.B. (1931). 'Transition'. In G.B. Shaw et al. *Fabian Essays in Socialism*. London: The Fabian Society and George Allen and Unwin, pp. 161–87.

Smaldone, W. (2014). *European Socialism: A Concise History with Documents*. Lanham, MD: Rowman and Littlefield.

Sperber, J. (2013). *Karl Marx: A Revolutionary Life*. New York: Livebright.

Stalin, J. (1928). *Leninism: Volume One*. London: George Allen and Unwin.

Stalin, J. (1972). *Economic Problems of Socialism in the USSR*. Peking: Foreign Languages Press.

Stears, M. (1998). 'Guild Socialism and Ideological Diversity on the British Left, 1914–1926', *Journal of Political Ideologies*, 3 (3): 289–307.

Stedman Jones, G. (2017). *Karl Marx: Greatness and Illusion*. London: Penguin.

Sternhell, Z. (1979). 'Fascist Ideology'. In W. Laqueur (ed.), *Fascism: A Reader's Guide*. Harmondsworth: Penguin, pp. 325–406.